Publish and be damned
www.pabd.com

Will the Real Mary Kelly...?

Christopher Scott

Publish and be damned
www.pabd.com

First published in Great Britain 2005 by Christopher Scott. The moral right of Christopher Scott to be identified as the author of this work has been asserted.

Designed in London, Great Britain, by Adlibbed Limited.
Printed and bound in the UK or the US.

ISBN: 1-905277-05-9

*To Chris Moverly, who taught me
the true meaning of friendship.*

Acknowledgements:
Many people have contributed to the writing of the present work by their help and support. But I feel that I must mention the following (in no particular order!) for their help and friendship, without which the writing of this work would have been infinitely more difficult, if not impossible. To all who have helped, my most grateful thanks!

Paul Begg
Stephen P. Ryder
Howard Brown
Neal Stubbings
Louis van Dompselaar

Sources:
The main sources used for the current work were:
Books:
The Jack the Ripper A-Z – Begg, Fido and Skinner
Jack the Ripper: The Mystery Solved – Paul Harrison
The Complete History of Jack the Ripper – Philip Sugden
Jack the Ripper: The Facts – Paul Begg
The Ripper and the Royals – Melvyn Fairclough
The Ultimate Jack the Ripper Sourcebook – Evans and Skinner
Jack the Ripper: The Simple Truth – Bruce Paley
Websites:
Casebook Jack the Ripper – http://www.casebook.org
http://www.ancestry.com
http://www.1837online.com
http://freebmd.rootsweb.com

Contents:

Introduction

In 1939, Winston Churchill famously described the Kremlin, and Russian foreign policy in general, as "a riddle wrapped in a mystery inside an enigma." These words could justifiably be applied also to Mary Jane Kelly, the last generally acknowledged victim of the Whitechapel murderer, the nameless, faceless man now known in perpetuity by the brutal sobriquet (which he almost certainly did not coin himself) of Jack the Ripper. It is indeed ironic that a young, unremarkable woman, who has achieved by the manner of her death an enduring immortality that surely would have astounded her in life, presents to the researcher seemingly intractable problems in discovering any tangible and provable facts about her life and background.

Mary Kelly was the last of the so called "canonical" victims, who are widely accepted to be five in number - Mary Ann Nichols, Annie Chapman, Elizabeth Stride, Catherine Eddowes and, finally, Kelly herself. The word "canonical" is derived from an analogy with the world of artistic works. In the fields of painting, literature, musical composition etc., those works which are generally accepted as provably the product of the hand to which they are attributed, constitute that artist's "canon" of work. It may seem bizarre that such savage and infamous killings as the Whitechapel murders should be compared to the products of high art, but the term is now firmly entrenched and it would seem unnecessarily pedantic to seek another. About all of the other four canonical victims we know a good deal with regard to their background and family and their history prior to their falling to the hand of the Whitechapel murderer. We have been able to trace many documentary references to these four women - for example, references in successive census returns, marriage certificates and birth certificates - and in the case of all these four killings, friends, family members and acquaintances came forward with provable testimony about the women. It should be added that of three of these first four victims - Nichols, Stride and Eddowes - we have only to date been able to gain some insight into their appearance from the mortuary photographs which were taken after they had succumbed to their dreadful end. Indeed, Annie Chapman is

11

the only one of the canonical victims for whom a photograph taken in life has come to light. This in itself is not particularly unusual or noteworthy. Although by 1888 photography could certainly not be described as still in its infancy, it is certainly not apparent that women of the social class and background of the Whitechapel victims would have had photographs taken as a matter of course. Of course, it is remotely possible that images taken in life of one of the victims may still lay neglected and unidentified. The photograph of Annie Chapman and her husband came to light only comparatively recently, so it certainly cannot be confidently claimed that all such material has yet emerged.

It must be said that Kelly is not the only possible victim who poses a problem with regard to documentary evidence. In July 1889, Alice McKenzie was found murdered in Castle Alley. She also has proved remarkably elusive when it comes to any provable references in the available records. Contemporary accounts of the case tell us only two things which may have led to some revelation of her background or previous history - that she was allegedly from Peterborough and was also known by the name of Bryant. Both items have thus far led nowhere. Other persons involved in the case of the Whitechapel murders about whom we would desperately like to know more have proved equally nebulous. Among the vast array of suspects whose names have emerged over the years of study and speculation, we would love to know more about Michael Ostrog and Nathan Kaminsky, and among the major witnesses involved, there is still disagreement among researchers about the firm documentary evidence of two of the most important, George Hutchinson and Joseph Barnett. Both of these witnesses became embroiled in the case specifically in relation to the Kelly murder, and we will hear more of both later.

So what material is available about Mary Jane Kelly? When the documentation and press reports relating to her murder are first perused, it would seem that we have a wealth of evidence, some of it extremely detailed. Friends and acquaintances of Mary came forward both at her inquest and more informally to press and police, and offered many alleged facts about her life and background. Central to all of these accounts, as we will discuss in more detail later, must stand the testimony of Joseph Barnett, with whom Kelly lived at various locations for a period of at least eighteen months prior to her murder. It was in the room which they had shared in Miller's Court, off the notorious Dorset Street, that Kelly met her death. However impressive and factual Barnett's testimony may appear at first sight, it has proved impervious to all research efforts to date. Not one of the "facts" itemised by Barnett has led to documentary confirmation. And herein lies the crux of the problem. Because so little is known about Kelly that can be proved - indeed, to all intents, nothing - she has become a blank canvas on which many later alleged accounts and theories have been written. It is indeed ironic that the Whitechapel victim about whom we know least has become the most discussed of them all.

In an entirely unscientific manner, I regard all these alleged facts and theories about Mary Kelly as falling into one of four categories:- feasible, possible, unlikely and barking mad! We will be seeing plenty of each type as we look at available accounts, both contemporary and later. In a highly unflattering comparison, the status of Kelly is rather like a ship that has lain wrecked on the sea bed since 1888. All the later concretions - some of which were spawned amazingly quickly after her death - have hidden, layer by successive layer, what little of the original outline we might once have been able to discern. I will be looking at police statements and accounts to see what, if anything, can be gleaned by way of fact with regard to the crime itself. The statements of her lover, friends and acquaintances - both at her controversial inquest and as reported in the press - will be examined with a critical eye to see if any of the assertions can be verified. Lastly, we will navigate the tortuous and often bizarre accounts of later theorists and writers who have invoked the name and presence of Kelly as a central figure in their account of and explanation for the murders and their perpetrator. What, if anything, can we truly say we know about this most famous and most elusive victim of Jack the Ripper?

Chapter 1

The Affair at Miller's Court

It is, perhaps, ironic that the only definite facts known about Mary Kelly, the most discussed and least documented of the victims of the Whitechapel murderer, are those which attend her death and its immediate aftermath. We will look in the first instance at those facts which the police investigation into the killing of Mary Kelly on the 9th November , 1888, and her inquest were able to elicit. For the moment we will abjure anything which may fall into the realms of hearsay or speculation in order to establish exactly what aspects of the murder and its investigation by the police authorities could fairly and reasonably be accepted as established fact. The theories, hearsay and speculation will, of course, be looked at in due course, but in order to put into perspective just how much or how little we truly know about Mary Kelly, it would seem appropriate to initially look at the established facts as a relatively secure base from which to proceed.

The principal event of the 9th November, 1888, should have been that yearly, colourful celebration of capitalism and pageantry which is the Lord Mayor's Show, marking the inauguration of the quaintly clad senior official of the City of London. This annual ritual has not only survived the intervening years but still occurs in early November and follows substantially the same route. More than five weeks had passed since the last killings in the Whitechapel area - the so called "double event" on the 30th of September - which had witnessed the murders of Elizabeth Stride and Catherine Eddowes. Whether the killer deliberately chose the day of the procession that marked the Lord Mayor's Show - knowing that many police officers would be occupied in duties connected with the event, or perversely wishing to steal the headlines from the event of the day - cannot, of course, be known. But this day in early November was to mark the final murder in the series which is generally agreed as being attributable to the same hand and certainly there would have been, as much as was possible under the shadow of the recent bloody events in Whitechapel, a comparatively festive atmosphere as, doubtless, many of the locals intended to get their fair share of the festivities.

The location of the events that were to unfold and deprive the Lord Mayor of his moment in the public eye, was a narrow, grimy cul de sac known as Miller's Court, which ran northwards off the infamous Dorset Street. The hair raising descriptions of Dorset Street in the heart of Spitalfields, which cast it as the most evil thoroughfare in London and virtually a "no go" area for the police authorities, may well be overstated and unduly dramatised. Certainly contemporary maps and census information show that the street contained a number of sizeable common lodging houses, such as that run by William Crossingham and the inhabitants of the street must at any given time have included a significant proportion of itinerant persons who used the common lodging houses for casual, short term accommodation. However, these same sources show that Dorset Street also contained a significant number of households with established, long term businesses and residents. We must not assume that all residents even of the common lodging houses were short term lodgers unknown to those who ran these establishments. There is evidence even within the documents relating to the Whitechapel murders to show that it was certainly not unknown for some residents of these houses to stay for months or even years, or to alternate between a small number of such establishments at need.

Miller's Court was essentially a short, blind alleyway with small houses to either side which were tenanted by a variety of households. A narrow arched entrance led into the court from the north side of Dorset Street. Access was gained between numbers 26 and 27 Dorset Street. The business located at Number 27 was a chandler's shop which was managed and run by one John McCarthy and his family. Evidence from a later murder often linked with the Whitechapel series, that of Alice McKenzie in Castle Alley, tells us that McCarthy's shop stayed open to a very late hour and also served food. As well as his business at Number 27, McCarthy was also the landlord of a certain number of properties which he let out. The exact number of such properties that he rented out has never been definitively established, but the properties in Miller's

Court were known colloquially as "McCarthy's Rents," so it seems reasonable to assume that at least a number of the properties in the court were let out by him. McCarthy also rented out rooms at 26 Dorset Street and over the course of time the internal layout of the house had been changed to provide more units for letting. Partition walls had been inserted and it was one of these changes which had created the room in which Mary Kelly had been living with Joseph Barnett since February or March of 1888. Although Kelly's room was designated as 13 Miller's Court, it was in effect the ground floor back room of 26 Dorset Street.

The room itself was a dismal, basic habitation which was approximately twelve feet square with a small fireplace. A single door led into the room from the arched alleyway that led into Miller's Court and two windows in the ground floor room looked out onto a bay in Miller's Court where a pump was situated. The furnishing was, as we would expect, sparse and basic - a bed with slatted base and turned pine headboard, two small tables, a washstand and chairs. The famous photograph of Kelly taken after death when the body was still in situ as found shows the partition wall of the room and the outline of a panel door can clearly be seen as forming part of this wall. Presumably at some stage this door, which must originally have led through to another part of number 26 which looked out on to Dorset Street, had been sealed up as part of the creation of this small room for rent.

At the time when the body was found in 13 Miller's Court, late in the morning of 9th November, two other facts must be mentioned which bear on the physical state of the room and its contents. The door which led into the room from the passageway outside was, for some reason, incapable of being opened. There has been much discussion about the absence of a key and its whereabouts, much theorising about how and why the door could not be opened in the normal way. But more of that later as it is not fact but speculation. The other relevant physical fact about the room was that at least one of the panes in the window nearer to the passageway was broken, and this broken glass was either covered with a curtain or had a wad of cloth stuffed into it.

The rent which Barnett and Kelly had been paying for the room was reported as four shillings and sixpence a week. To put this into perspective, the normal charge for a bed at a common lodging house was fourpence per night for a single bed and eightpence for a double. So, by way of comparison, if Kelly and Barnett had lived at one of the lodging houses in Dorset Street, they would have paid fifty six pence per week for their bed, or four shillings and eightpence. It has been argued that it is difficult to see how a couple in the situation of Kelly and Barnett could afford a room at such a rent, but in fact it worked out marginally cheaper than living in a lodging house. John McCarthy claimed at Kelly's inquest that the couple were in arrears with their rent to the sum of twenty nine shillings, and that the rent was due and was paid weekly. This raises two main questions which are 1) Why would a businessman such as McCarthy who operated within the financially precarious environment of the East End, allow such arrears to accrue and 2) why do the arrears amount to such an odd sum? The first of these will be looked at when we come to consider the possible relationship between Kelly and McCarthy. The second question hinges on the simple fact that the arrears due is not divisible by the weekly rent. If the rent were 4/6 per week then six weeks rent would have amounted to 27 shillings. So all we can say with certainty is that somewhere in excess of six weeks rent was unpaid. The most likely reason for the odd amount is that as Kelly lived yards from McCarthy's shop, and presumably did at least some of her day to day shopping there, it is possible that McCarthy extended to her, as one of his tenants, a small amount of credit. But again this is in the realm of speculation. What must be remembered is that twenty nine shillings in the East End was a considerable amount of money and does seem an unusually large amount for McCarthy to allow persons of the social and financial status of Kelly and Barnett to run up.

However, it was the rent arrears that led to the body being discovered in Kelly's room at 13 Miller's Court. McCarthy employed a man most commonly named as Thomas Bowyer, but also listed variously as John or Harry Bowyer and known by the nickname of "Indian Harry." We are told that he was an army pensioner, but to date all searches for more information on Bowyer have proved fruitless. At Kelly's inquest he gave his address as 37 Dorset Street, which was not one of the large common lodging houses located in the street. In 1881 it was occupied by two Jewish families, the Beliskys and the Jacobs, and a Spitalfields family by the name of Fox. In 1891 the occupancy of the house had been taken by four Jewish families of the names of Brooks, York, Donovan and Burns. One of these residents, John Donovan, was listed as a fish porter. Late on the morning of the 9th of November, at approximately 10.45, McCarthy instructed Bowyer to go to Kelly's room and see if he could get any of the outstanding rent. We do not know on what day Kelly's rent would normally have been due or how often Bowyer, or McCarthy himself, had visited Kelly in the period immediately prior to the murder to try and get the outstanding rent money. The fact that Bowyer did not accept the failure of Kelly to answer as proof that she was not in may suggest that he had already had experience of her hiding from the rent man, which must have been a common occurrence in the East End of the time. Bowyer went round to the broken window, of which he was presumably aware, and pulled back the cloth or curtain. As his eyes adjusted to the comparative gloom within the room, he saw first the portions of Kelly's body on the table beside the bed and then the body itself. One can only imagine the effect that the sight of this ghastly shambles had on Bowyer and it must surely have stayed with him to the end of his days. He ran off to get McCarthy who returned with him and the landlord looked through the broken pane himself. McCarthy and Bowyer went to the Commercial Street police station to report what they had found and the police inspector on duty returned with them. There have over the years been various claims by certain police officers that they were first on the scene of the Miller's Court murder. This dubious honour, as reported at the inquest, actually belonged to Walter Beck who was on duty when McCarthy reported the murder.

This is where things start to get complicated. The sequence of events that followed the reporting of the murder in Miller's Court has been variously characterised as a bungling fiasco, an understandably cautious effort by the police to maximise the evidential leads at the scene of the crime, or simply a breakdown in police communications. The truth probably lies, as usual, somewhere in the middle. The timetable of the major players, as reported at the inquest, informs us that the murder was reported to Beck at Commercial Street police station just after 11 o'clock. He appears to have taken the following actions - to notify Dr. Phillips, the divisional police surgeon, and require him to attend the scene, to request the attendance of bloodhounds, whose use had been widely urged and argued about and for which trials had been held under the supervision of Charles Warren, the Metropolitan Police Commissioner, and, presumably, Beck also notified Inspector Abberline of the events in hand. Beck immediately went to Miller's Court with McCarthy and Bowyer and sealed the court off. Allowing for the time to quickly make the arrangements outlined above and for the time required to get to Miller's Court, Beck must have arrived at somewhere about 11.10. Dr. Phillips states in his inquest testimony that he arrived at the scene of the murder at 11.15 and Abberline got there at 11.30. The breakdown in police communications referred to amounted to the fact that not only were the bloodhounds, whose services had been mooted, not available for loan to the police, they were not even still in London. This, coupled with the fact that the door to 13 Miller's Court could not readily be opened without undue force, led to a considerable delay before Kelly's room was entered.

Dr. Phillips made what observations he could by simply looking through the window from the court and satisfied himself that there was no one in the room who could benefit from immediate medical attention. The doctor reported at the inquest that he remained at the scene until it was finally decided to force entry into Kelly's room. This action was taken at 1.30 in the afternoon. The chain of command in this situation is interesting. Abberline testified that the suggestion to leave the door closed until the dogs arrived came from Dr. Phillips. Word was finally brought that the dogs would not be coming with the arrival at 1.30 of Superintendent Arnold who was the officer who actually ordered the door to be forced. One can only imagine the atmosphere and the conversation during that period of over two hours while those involved stood around in Miller's Court waiting. It must have seemed endless. One wonders how many ventured a look through that broken window, how large were the crowds that built up in Dorset Street, and what rumours were flying around the residents of Miller's Court who were effectively trapped in their own homes.

Once the door had been forced - Phillips says by McCarthy himself - the doctor entered the room and carried out a preliminary examination of the body. This would have been required to formally certify death - not that there was much doubt on that count - but also to see what observations of value could be made by examining the body in situ. In his inquest testimony Phillips reconstructs what he considers to be the sequence of events that attended the woman's death. The body, as found, lay on the side of the bed nearer the door, i.e. the right hand side as viewed from the foot of the bed. But Phillips opined from the pattern and distribution of blood both on and under the bed that the fatal cut to the woman's throat had actually been effected with her lying on the other side of the bed, nearer the partition wall. The body had, in his opinion, been moved after death to where it was found. Phillips reports that there was saturation with blood at the corner nearest the wall of the palliasse (i.e. the mattress), the pillow and the sheet and was even specific enough to say that the immediate cause of death was the severing of the right carotid artery. If these observations are correct they raise some interesting issues. The severance of the right carotid artery with the body in the position that Phillips suggests would mean that the right hand side of Kelly's body was hard against the partition wall. If the killer severed the throat either astride the body or leaning over it, then this would strongly suggest that the killer was right handed, as a left handed cut in this position would be well nigh impossible. The question as to why the body was moved after the throat was cut could either confirm the handedness of the killer - ask any right handed person which side of a double bed they prefer! - or that the killer wished to pose the body to allow maximum access for the subsequent mutilations.

As well as Phillips, in his capacity as divisional surgeon, a team of medics attended the scene of the crime. Dr. Bond, Dr. Browne and Dr. Gabe are also noted as being present. Before any examination was made the now famous photographs of Kelly's body on the bed were taken. The next major arrival was Robert Anderson, the Assistant Commissioner, who is reported to have arrived by cab at 1.50 p.m. The medical men were engaged in their examination at the scene for almost two and a half hours, finishing shortly after 4 p.m. At that point the remains of Kelly were removed in a covered van and conveyed to the Shoreditch mortuary. Inspector Abberline examined the room at 13 Miller's Court and among the meagre group of objects found noted half a candle and a pipe. The inspector also observed that what appeared to have been a substantial fire had burned in the grate, and what appeared to have been clothing had been incinerated and a portion of the wire frame of a woman's bonnet was found. Abberline noted that the spout of the kettle had melted. The ashes from the grate were subsequently sifted carefully, but nothing of note was discovered. This conflagration in Kelly's room has been much discussed and will be examined in more detail later.

After Kelly's remains were removed to the Shoreditch Mortuary, there remained the harrowing matter of the full post mortem. Although Kelly's body was given unprecedented attention in situ, with a bevy of medics examining the body for somewhere in the region of two and a half hours before it was deemed ready to be moved from the room at Miller's Court, a full and detailed post mortem was conducted at the mortuary. Although Dr. Phillips was the doctor initially summoned by the police and was the first on the scene, the post mortem, although attended by a group of medical men, was carried out and the report on it written up by Dr. Thomas Bond. The detailed post mortem report, which was missing for many years but was finally returned anonymously to Scotland Yard, is dated the 16th of November, but this was obviously not the date on which it was performed. Another document penned by Dr. Bond, commonly referred to as the "profile", in which Bond compares each murder in the series and draws certain conclusions about the killer, makes it clear that the post mortem was actually carried out on the day of the murder. This document is dated the 10th of November and Bond refers to the post mortem that he carried out on the Dorset Street victim "yesterday."

The post mortem report of Thomas Bond laid certain myths to rest.

Even until the late 1980's it was frequently stated that Kelly had been pregnant at the time of her death, whilst, in direct contradiction, certain contemporary press reports stated, or more often hinted, that Kelly's uterus had been excised and taken by the killer, whilst other reports at the time were adamant that the post mortem showed that no bodily parts were missing. When Bond's report became available for study, it was stated that this showed that the killer did appear to have taken a "trophy" but in Kelly's case it was the heart. It was even theorised that it was the woman's heart which had been burnt in the fire. The interpretation of what Bond actually intended to convey hinges on the use of one word. In the post mortem report, the doctor simply says "the pericardium was open below and the heart absent." In my opinion this is only open to one interpretation, namely that the killer excised and took the heart away. Theories about the organ being burnt on the fire or boiled up in the kettle simply do not stand up to examination in the light of Abberline's unequivocal statement that the fire and its contents attracted specific attention and were carefully and systematically examined. The statement of Bond is also interesting in that the killer did not simply excise the organ but removed it via an opening in the lower part of the pericardium. This is a membranous sac filled with fluid which surrounds the heart and is divided into three layers. It serves to limit the motion of the heart, serves as a shock absorber and prevents the heart from overexpanding when blood volume increases. The logical "cut off points" for the heart would be the major artery and vein located at the top of the organ, so to remove it from below whist leaving the pericardium intact would have been no easy feat.

The details of Bond's post mortem make disturbing and uncomfortable reading, even to a reader in an age when we are supposed to be desensitised to violence and gore. Kelly had been utterly dehumanised and virtually disassembled. The doctor commences his report with a detailed summary of the position in which the body was found as can be seen in the famous photograph taken at Miller's Court. Bond then lists the physical condition of the body as it was found and the disposition of the various body parts as the killer had placed them around the room. Bond listed the following as the major areas which had been subject to mutilation:

1) The surface of the thighs had been removed
2) The surface of the abdomen had been removed and the contents thereof extracted
3) The arms bore several jagged wounds
4) The face had been mutilated beyond recognition
5) The tissues of the neck had been cut down to the vertebrae

The killer had placed (which does not imply any ritualistic motive) the body parts about the room as follows:

1) The uterus, both kidneys and one breast were under the head
2) The second breast was by the right foot
3) The liver was between the feet
4) The intestines were by the right side
5) The spleen was by the left side of the body
6) The surface tissues from the thighs and the abdomen were on the table beside the bed.

The first fact that is apparent is that not all the bodily parts are accounted for. The lungs and the major part of the stomach were in situ but, as well as the comment Bond makes later about the heart, he makes it clear that the abdomen was entirely emptied but such a major organ as the bladder is not mentioned or listed. Although Kelly's body had been so grossly abused the post mortem was reported in the press as including, as in the case of the Chapman murder, the replacing of the body parts back in their natural positions within the body cavity. As part of the bladder had been removed in the case of Chapman, the fact that this organ is simply not mentioned in Kelly's post mortem is surprising. As the document we are looking at in this case is not a press report which might be expected to edit or summarise such findings, but the full post mortem report itself, this omission is hard to explain.

Anything further in connection with the Kelly murder is either speculation, more or less informed, hearsay or sheer fantasy. The degree of dissension concerning Mary Jane Kelly and the purported facts surrounding her life and death is astounding. Apart from the more outlandish legends and versions of reality which have arisen, which we examine later, even the more mundane aspects of this singular murder and its background cannot be agreed upon. Can we truly know anything about the background and character of Kelly? What were her movements immediately prior to the killing? Was it, indeed, Mary Jane Kelly who was killed at Miller's Court? What was her real name? Was Kelly the last victim of the Whitechapel murderer? Upon none of these questions is there any degree of concensus. We will now look at these and other mysteries in turn and see what light, if any, can be thrown into these dark corners.

Chapter 2

Who Died at Miller's Court?

The most fundamental question, surely, that we must address is this - was the body found at 13 Miller's Court on the morning of the 9th of November, 1888, really that of the woman known to her lover, neighbours and landlord as Mary Jane Kelly? If the victim was not Kelly then, of course, all the speculation and attempted research into her background is superfluous except for esoteric, academic interest. We certainly cannot dismiss this possibility out of hand as the idea that the body in the room at Miller's Court was not Mary Kelly is not that new and is certainly still alive and well. Indeed, in one of the most recent outings of the Whitechapel murders as popular entertainment, the high profile film "From Hell," starring Johnny Depp, Mary Kelly survives the affair at Miller's Court and makes her way back to an idyllic cottage on the coast of Ireland. However, it has to be said that this particular version of events is by no means the most bizarre interpretation of the Whitechapel murders to be found in this film. The question of Kelly's survival or otherwise, really splits down into three lines of inquiry. What possible reason or reasons could have given rise to the idea that Kelly did not die on the 9th of November? If the body found that morning was not that of the woman known as Mary Kelly, then who was it? And, finally, if Kelly did not die that day, what happened to her?

The identification of the body as that of Kelly is complex and involved a number of individuals. In the days before fingerprints, DNA testing and the forensic use of dental records, the principal means of identification would have been simply by facial recognition or any distinguishing marks. Joseph Barnett, who had lived with Kelly for about eighteen months according to his police statement, stated in his inquest testimony, "I have seen the body. I identify her by the ear and eyes. I am positive it is the same woman." Two things must be noted here. It may seem odd that Barnett felt the need to say that he was positive it was Kelly. However, it must be remembered that the facial disfigurement carried out on the corpse found at Miller's Court was so

25

gross and so extensive as to render any identification less than certain, even more so for a casual acquaintance than for the lover with whom she had been living. Dr. Bond in his post mortem report summarises the facial mutilations as follows:

"The face was gashed in all directions, the nose, the cheeks, eyebrows and ears being partly removed. The lips were blanched and cut by several oblique incisions running obliquely down to the chin. There were also numerous cuts extending regularly across all the features."

If one looks at the face as shown on the well known photograph of the corpse in situ in Miller's Court, it is hard to recognise it as human, let alone confidently identify it as that of a particular individual. It has struck some as odd that Barnett said he recognised Kelly by the ear and the eyes. As Bond specifically states that the eyebrows had been partly excised the eyes would presumably have been identifiable only if they were particularly striking, as, for example, they had been in life of an unusual colour. However, we must remember that Barnett had been Kelly's companion and lover for eighteen months, so if anyone were well placed to recognise her from one single feature, he would presumably have been best qualified to do so. It has also been noted as odd by some that Barnett would say he identified the corpse by the ear, especially as Bond specifically says that the ears were partly removed. Whether Barnett had a particular penchant for, or even a fetish for, any single feature of Kelly's we cannot, of course, say. One explanation put forward for this seemingly odd statement is that Barnett was misreported and had actually said that he identified the corpse by the eyes and the hair. However, on the question of misreporting or mishearing evidence, it is worth noting that this testimony of Barnett is taken not from a press report, wherein the evidence would be quoted as edited by a reporter, but from the official inquest papers which are held at the Greater London Record Office. One would reasonably expect the possibility of misreporting in such a source to be less than in a newspaper article. Certainly it would seem logical that the hair of the corpse, which can be clearly seen in the Miller's Court photograph, would have been a more prominent and more intact feature to serve as a basis for recognition, but we have no firm grounds on the basis of the inquest papers for thinking that Barnett said anything other than the words he is reported as uttering.

John McCarthy, Kelly's landlord, in his inquest testimony, is quoted as saying, "I knew the deceased as Mary Jane Kelly. I have seen the body and have no doubt as to the identity." McCarthy's meaning here is not entirely clear in that we cannot be sure whether he meant he identified the body from what he saw of it at Miller's Court, or whether he subsequently went to the mortuary and made a formal identification there. We cannot know how closely McCarthy was able to see the corpse in situ as it lay on the bed. When the murder was first drawn to his attention and the two looked at the ghastly scene through the broken pane, it seems certain they could not make a firm identification. It may be significant that Bowyer, in his inquest testimony, says only, "I saw a body of some one laid on the bed, and blood on the floor." It was reported that when the room was finally broken into by forcing the door at 1.30 p.m., it was McCarthy who actually carried out the deed. It may have been that the police were deferring to McCarthy the right to break into his own property, but it seems unlikely they would have worried about such niceties faced with such a gross murder which would surely have occupied all their attention. However, it is not reported whether McCarthy actually went into the room with the officers and the doctor. Thinking through the practicalities of any number of people trying to move carefully around a scene of crime in a room barely twelve feet square which contained at least a bed, table and washstand, the presence of any person other than those strictly needed seems unlikely. Indeed, it seems likely that in such a strictly confined space the group of medical men would have been given first access to carry out their initial examination, even before Abberline and other officers searched the room for anything of significance. This leads to the conclusion that it is likely that McCarthy went to the mortuary to make a formal identification.

In both the cases of Barnett and McCarthy - and, indeed, in the case of any others who went to formally view the body - we have to wonder what state the corpse was in when it was identified. It was reported that as part of the formal process at the mortuary the team of medics reassembled, as far as was possible, the body parts which were retrieved from Miller's Court. What we are not told was whether any facial reconstruction or stitching was carried out. We know from one of the post mortem photographs of Catherine Eddowes that this was done in her case. But as the only existing photograph of Kelly's face was taken before her remains were conveyed to Shoreditch Mortuary, we cannot know whether this was done in Kelly's case. Even had this been done, the face would still have been a dreadful sight, but without this it would have been truly ghastly.

A third person who, we are told, was required to go to the mortuary and identify Kelly's body was George Hutchinson, whose statement, which has caused endless debate and speculation, we will discuss more fully later. However, he came forward too late, unfortunately, to be called to give evidence at the inquest. In fact, Hutchinson actually came forward on the evening of the same day on which the inquest was held, the 12th of November. Hutchinson himself makes no mention of the identification in his own statement, but there is a surviving report by Inspector Abberline which details his interview with Hutchinson. After a brief resume of the contents of Hutchinson's evidence, Abberline adds, "he has promised to go with an officer tomorrow morning at 11.30 a.m. to the Shoreditch Mortuary to identify the deceased." As Hutchinson did not report to the police until 6 p.m. on the day on which the inquest concluded and the jury had delivered its verdict, it is interesting that Abberline felt the need for this witness, whom he considered credible and important, to make a further identification. It may, of course, have been a standard formality. Hutchinson claimed to have known Kelly for three years - longer than Barnett and, as far as we know, longer than McCarthy - so his identification would possibly carry more weight.

So, if three people who knew Kelly well - in the cases of Barnett and McCarthy, very well - identified the body found in the room at Miller's Court as that of Kelly, what possible grounds would there have been to doubt that the victim was exactly who she appeared to be? It should be noted as a most important point that there is no contemporary account, or even near contemporary account, which casts the slightest doubt on Kelly being the victim. Although there is frequent confusion about Kelly's name, which we shall discuss later, the assertion that the victim was the tenant of Room 13 was made in every account that I have seen published, most of them actually giving the name - or one of the confused variants which are evidently referring to the woman we know as Mary Jane Kelly - in reports published the very day after the murder, the 10th of November, 1888. If there were any credibility in the later idea that the victim in the room was not Kelly, we would need to ask one pertinent question. Was this alleged killing of another woman in Kelly's room the result of some unfathomable plot on the part of some unknown party, or was it a hideous coincidental accident whereby a woman who happened to be in Kelly's room when the Ripper came calling was killed in her stead?

If it were not Kelly in that squalid room, then who could it have been? Much has been made of the fact that it was reported that Kelly had been giving a roof and a bed to at least one, possibly two female acquaintances in the period shortly before the Miller's Court murder. Indeed, this was, according to Joseph Barnett's account of events during those crucial days, the very circumstance that precipitated him to leave Kelly on the 30th of October. In his inquest testimony he is quite explicit as to why - "I left her because she had a person who was a prostitute whom she took in, and I objected to her doing so, that was the only reason." Barnett does not name this friend or acquaintance taken in by Kelly. He also reports that on the last occasion he saw Kelly alive, on the evening of the Thursday before the murder, there was "a female" there with him and Kelly. At the inquest the testimony of Maria Harvey casts some light on the matter. Harvey gave her address as New Court, which was a small cul de sac that ran parallel to Miller's Court slightly further along Dorset Street. Maria Harvey testified - "I slept two nights with her on Monday and Tuesday nights last I slept with her. We were together all the afternoon on Thursday - I was in the room when Joe Barnett called I went away." Harvey is clearly "the female" that Barnett referred to as being with Kelly on the Thursday evening, but was she also "the prostitute" whose presence caused him to leave? She referred to herself in her evidence as being a laundress and the detailed list of clothing she claimed to have left in Kelly's room lends credence to this.

Mention has also been made of a woman specifically identified as a prostitute who had been staying with Kelly during this period before the murder. She is referred to only as "Julia" and in one press source is described as German. An informant named Maurice Lewis told the press that he saw Kelly, Julia and a man he named as "Danny" drinking together on the evening leading up to the murder. However it should be noted both that Lewis' information is contained in a press report - he did not give evidence at the inquest and thus his information was not subject to scrutiny and cross examination - and that Barnett, both in his police statement and his inquest testimony, did not name the woman who had been staying with Kelly. However, in his statement to the police, Barnett suggests that the woman who had been staying with Kelly had led to an unwelcome return to Mary Jane's former way of life. Barnett makes no bones about how she had earned her living before they met - "She told me that she had obtained her livelihood as a prostitute for some considerable time before I took her from the streets." In this same statement it is clear that the circumstances of the couple, including, presumably, Kelly's unwelcome guest, had led her back to her old ways - "in consequence of not earning sufficient money to give her and her resorting to prostitution I resolved on leaving her." It has been suggested that this "Julia" who stayed with Kelly can be identified with a witness at the inquest named Julia Venturney. Apart from the name, there is not the slightest basis for this alleged identification. Julia Venturney, whose maiden name was Julia Cook, was most certainly not German and there is no justification whatever from her testimony, or from any other known source, for believing that she was a prostitute. In her deposition she said she was a charwoman who lived at No 1 Miller's Court with a man named Harry Owen. Far from being a candidate to be the woman who had stayed with Kelly, she gave further credence that there was another individual involved. She stated - "I last saw her (Kelly) alive on Thursday about 10 a.m. having her breakfast with another woman in her own room."

It is not easy to determine to what extent, if any, the women in Miller's Court who gave evidence were engaged in active or casual prostitution themselves. It has been claimed that the comings and goings in the course of the night and early morning prior to the murder suggest that some of these women may well have been walking the streets looking for business. Certainly by the standards of modern practices and habits these late night excursions do seem odd, even suspicious. The most likely candidate to be actively involved on the streets is Mary Ann Cox, who lived at No. 5, Miller's Court. She described herself as follows - "I am a widow - I get my living on the streets as best I can." This is not tantamount to an admission of being a prostitute, but on her police statement she is more explicit and says, "I am a widow and an unfortunate." The term "unfortunate" is by far the most common Victorian euphemism for "prostitute" - some others being "low women," "loose women," "sisters of joy," and many others. Her movements that night seem to our eyes odd to say the least. She returned to her home on the night of the murder at about midnight, but only remained for about fifteen minutes and then went out again. She returned at about 1 a.m., warmed her hands and then ventured out once more. She finally returned at about 3 a.m., but even then did not sleep and sat up fully dressed. Mary Cox did not venture to say in her inquest testimony where these nocturnal jaunts took her, nor did the cross examination raise this matter with her. However, on this point a little caution must be exercised and modern working and sleeping patterns must not be overlaid onto a very different period. In the testimony relating to the other victims there can be found examples of both men and women out on the streets at times which we would now find unusual. Social and work habits were very different and we must not let ourselves be led into making unjustified comparisons. Although it would not come as a huge surprise to find definitive proof (if such were ever possible) that some of the women who lived in Miller's Court were engaged in casual prostitution, we cannot say, except in the case of Mary Cox, that such a conclusion seems probable.

The women who lived in or were about Miller's Court who gave police or inquest statements are as follows:

1) Mary Ann Cox, 5 Miller's Court. She admitted to being an "unfortunate." Her movements on the night of the murder are outlined above.

2) Elizabeth Prater, Room 20, Miller's Court (her police statement gives her address as Room 20, 27 Dorset Street, but this is clearly a mistake, as this was the premises at which McCarthy lived and ran his chandler's business.) She lived in the room above Kelly at the back of 26 Dorset Street and said she had been standing at the entrance to the court until about 1.30 a.m. as she was waiting for a man she lived with who did not arrive. Who this man was has never been established. She went to bed shortly after 1.30 but was awakened, by her estimation, at some time between 3.30 and 4.00 by what she described as "screams of murder in a female voice." During Prater's vigil at the end of the passageway leading to the court she stood talking for some time to McCarthy. It may seem an ungodly hour for tenant and landlord to be standing chatting on the corner but premises such as McCarthy's stayed open to what seems to modern eyes an amazingly late hour. We have direct evidence in the testimony given regarding the finding of the body of Alice McKenzie in Castle Alley in July 1889. The body was found at about 12.50 a.m. and the constable who came upon the corpse encountered almost immediately a young man named Isaac Jacobs, plate in hand, off to get his supper. He specifically said that he was off to McCarthy's in Dorset Street.

3) Sarah Lewis, of Great Pearl Street, came over to stay at 2 Miller's Court with the Keylers owing to a domestic dispute. She arrived at the court between 2 and 3 a.m., heard a single cry of murder shortly before four o'clock and left the court at 5.30 p.m.

4) Julia Venturney, Room 1, Miller's Court. (See above.) She went to bed at 8 p.m. but only dozed all night. She heard no screams.

5) Maria Harvey, New Court. She stayed with Kelly on the nights of Monday the 5th and Tuesday the 6th November. She last saw Kelly at about 7 p.m. on the evening before the murder.

There seems little doubt that in the period immediately prior to Barnett leaving and the days leading up to the murder that Kelly was again engaged in prostitution. Barnett was out of work at the time of their separation and this was presumably a contributing factor to Kelly taking to the streets again. But if she had taken to active soliciting the arrears that had continued to accrue with McCarthy show that her earnings were only sufficient for the basics of life.

So the sequence of events is, to put it mildly, confused. Barnett testified that he left Kelly on the 30th of October, that is the Tuesday of the week before the murder. This was because she had taken in a woman that Barnett knew to be a prostitute, and he objected. Of course, we cannot know how long this other woman stayed with them before he decided he had to leave. Barnett has emerged in recent years as a keenly argued and enthusiastically championed suspect, at least for the murder of Kelly, if not the other four canonical victims. However, if we put ourselves into his place for a moment, and try to think through the practicalities of the situation in which he found himself, if his testimony is true, it would have tried the patience of the most saintly of men. Out of work, short of money, seeing the woman with whom he had shared his life going without, knowing or suspecting that she was again resorting to the streets for money - a test for any man. The domestic and sexual practicalities of two women and one man sharing a single room twelve feet square with one bed, can be imagined. One intriguing question is why Kelly took this other woman in. There have been speculations about some torrid lesbian affair in which Kelly was involved, but that remains entirely without basis. There may have been a desperately practical reason - with Barnett out of work, any extra money coming into the household would have been welcome. Kelly must surely have known or guessed the effect this unwanted guest would have on her relationship with Barnett, but her motives are, sadly, irrecoverable. The crucial question for the current argument is who was this other woman? If the mysterious "Julia", said to be German, was the lodger in question, she has never been identified. Whoever she was, she had apparently left by the beginning of the week of the murder, because Maria Harvey slept in Room 13 with Kelly on Monday and Tuesday of that week, and would surely have mentioned the presence of a third person.

So, if it were to be seriously argued that the body found on the 9th of November was not that of Kelly, then the only feasible possibility would be that it was that of her unfortunate visitor. This can only realistically be the mysterious Julia or Maria Harvey. As Harvey gave evidence at the inquest, we can safely discount her! If "Julia" did exist - which seems to me less than certain - it is apparent that she was no longer boarding with Kelly during the week of the murder. Barnett mentioned "a female" who was with Kelly in the room when he visited her the evening before the murder, the Thursday. Harvey's account makes it clear that it was she who was meant. At the inquest she said, "I was in the room when Joe Barnett called, I went away." Barnett said, "There was a female with us on Thursday evening when we were together. She left first and I left shortly afterwards." Why Barnett referred to Harvey as "a female" when he must have known her and she was in the room where the inquest was held with him, is not known. The only other female reported in Kelly's presence immediately prior to the murder is the one seen by Julia Venturney having breakfast with Kelly at 10 a.m. on the Thursday morning. Maria Harvey testified that she and Kelly were together all the Thursday afternoon, so it seems likely that the balance of probability is that Harvey was the woman seen by Venturney in Kelly's room.

Mention must be made of another alleged witness who claimed to have spent time with Kelly on the evening of the Thursday, 8 November. Her name is given as Lizzie Albrook or Allbrook and her age at the time of the murder as 20 years old. Although she was not called to testify at the Kelly inquest, her story was reported in at least three press sources, namely The Western Mail, Lloyd's Weekly and the St. James's Gazette. The bare facts of her statement read as follows in the St. James's Gazette version which appeared in the issue of the 12th of November, 1888:

"Lizzie Allbrook, a young woman of twenty, who resides in Miller's-court and works at a lodging-house in Dorset-street, says:-

I knew Mary Jane Kelly very well, as we were near neighbours. The last time I saw her was on Thursday night, about eight o'clock, when I left her in her room with Joe Barnett,the man who had been living with her. About the last thing she said to me was, "Whatever you do, don't you do wrong and turn out as I have." She had often spoken to me in this way, and warned me against going on the streets, as she had done. She told me, too, she was heartily sick of the life she was leading, and wished she had money enough to go back to Ireland, where her people lived. I don't believe she would have gone out as she did if she had not been obliged to do so in order to keep herself from starvation. She had talked to me about her friends several times, and on one occasion told me she had a female relation in London who was on the stage."

This testimony is highly interesting but raises various problems. The first, and arguably most important, is the verification of Lizzie Allbrook's identity. If her age as given in the press accounts is correct she would have been born in 1868, or, if born very late in the year, in 1867. However, across all four census returns from 1871 to 1901 inclusive, there is simply no record which is identifiable with such an individual. This is allowing for the fact that her name may have been listed under the form of Elizabeth, Eliza or even Louisa. It must also be remembered that is she were 20 years old in 1888 she may well have been married by then and, consequently, would not have appeared under the name Albrook or Allbrook in the censuses for 1871 and 1881. However, we would expect her to be listed under her married name in 1891 and 1901 but this is not the case. The only Allbrook of approximately the right age with any connection to Whitechapel is a 15 year old girl listed in the 1881 census who was in service to a household in Lancashire:

1881:

Gassyard Hall, Caton, Lancashire

Head: Constance Edmonson aged 49 born Caton - Income from Land

Sisters:

Margaret Edmondson aged 48 born Quernmore, Lancashire

Lula C Edmondson aged 40 born Sidmouth, Devon

Servants:

Margaret Black aged 35 born Allonby, Cumberland

Louisa Albrook aged 15 born Whitechapel, London.

However, on tracing this young lady in 1891, she is still resident in Lancashire, albeit with a different household.

If we try to trace Allbrook using her initial (on the supposition this was L. or E.) then we do find an interesting entry in the 1901 census.

1 Flower and Dean Street

Head: W S Allbrook aged 33 born Mile End - Dock labourer

Wife: E J Allbrook aged 32 born Spitalfields

Sons:

W S Allbrook aged 10 born Bethnal Green
H J Allbrook aged 5 born Hoxton
Daughter:
A D R Allbrook aged 7 months born Spitalfields
We can trace with some certainty the births of all three children. The son W.S. was the William Allbrook whose birth was registered in March 1891. The son H.J. was very probably the Henry Thomas Allbrook registered in Bethnal Green in March 1896. The daughter A.D.R. was Annie Rose Allbrook and her birth was registered in Whitechapel in December 1900. The name of this couple may well have been Holbrook as a listing closly resembling them is detailed as follows in the 1891 census:

59 Old Nicholl Street, Bethnal Green, London:
Head:
William Holbrook aged 25 born Bethnal Green - Carman
Wife: Emma Holbrook aged 22 born Bethnal Green.
Children:
Emma aged 2
William aged 2 months
Both children born in Bethnal Green
I have been unable to trace the birth of a William Holbrook in Bethnal Green in the first quarter of 1891. This may well be the same William Allbrook registered in the same period and location. However, if the E.J. Allbrook of 1901 is the same as the Emma Holbrook of 1891, then identification with her as Lizzie Allbrook seems unlikely. If her forename had been Eliza then this could reasonably have been argued.

The most potent objection to Allbrook's testimony, in my opinion, is on logical and evidential grounds. Two of the witnesses at the Kelly inquest mentioned this crucial period of the evening of the 8th November, namely, Joseph Barnett and Maria Harvey. Barnett said that on that evening he saw Kelly between 7.30 and 7.45 p.m. and he was with her about one hour. While he was with Kelly there was a "female" there also who left shortly before him. Maria Harvey testified that she was with Kelly on the Thursday evening when Barnett arrived after which she left. Although there is a discrepancy over the time, these two testimonies match so closely and there is no mention by any witness of a supernumerary female with Kelly. It seems unlikely that if both Allbrook and Harvey had been present at varying times when Barnett saw Kelly that he would not have mentioned it. Everything suggests to me that Allbrook's quoted tale is simply a version of Maria Harvey's evidence. Similar confusion arose in an earlier case, the murder of Annie Chapman, over the identities of the witnesses Mrs. Darrell and Mrs. Long. If Lizzie Allbrook did exist she may have known Kelly but all the evidence suggests that she was not in Kelly's room at the time of Barnett's visit on the evening of the 8th November.

All of the above observations convince me that there is no credible reason to believe that the body found at 13 Miller's Court was other than that of the woman known as Mary Jane Kelly. It seems that accounts of the events which incorporate the supposition of Kelly's survival put the interpretation before the facts. It cannot be that any such theory is based on sustainable evidence for Kelly's not dying on the 9th November - there simply is none. Rather, in my opinion, a story is woven which, for its fabric to hold together, requires Kelly's survival as a given fact and it therefore becomes a self proving hypothesis. Therefore, the third question posed at the beginning of this section - what happened to Kelly if she survived? - becomes meaningless. There have been some wonderful and picturesque versions - such as the plot of "From Hell" already mentioned - which require Kelly to survive and, metaphorically, to ride off into the sunset. As long as these versions are clearly seen as fiction then I do not have any problem with them and can enjoy them as entertainment as well as the next man. It is when they are presented as fact, or as a viable theory of the historical events, that I feel the need to point out that they are built on foundations of sand.

Chapter 3

The Conventional Account of Mary Kelly's Life

By far the most detailed and discussed version of the events in the life of Mary Jane Kelly is that provided by Joseph Barnett. Although odd details are provided by other testimony, such as that of Mrs. Carthy, John McCarthy, an unnamed missionary and others - all of which will be discussed in due course - it is hardly surprising that the fullest account would come from the man with whom Kelly had been living with, effectively as a common law husband, for about eighteen months. The alleged details are contained in two documents, namely Barnett's statement to the police dated the 9th of November, the day of the murder, and his inquest deposition as contained in the papers relating to this inquiry. In his police statement Barnett stated:

"The deceased told me one occasion that her father named John Kelly was a foreman at some iron works at lived at Carmarthen or Carnarvon, that she had a brother named Henry serving in 2nd. Battn. Scots Guards, and known amongst his comrades as Johnto, and I believe the regiment is now in Ireland. She also told me that she had obtained her livelihood as a prostitute for some considerable time before I took her from the streets, and that she left her home about 4 years ago, and that she was married to a collier, who was killed through some explosion. I think she said her husband's name was Davis or Davies." (Note that the peculiar grammatical construction in the first sentence is present in the original.)

In his inquest testimony Barnett expands considerably the amount of detail about Kelly's former life:

"Her name was Marie Jeanette Kelly. Kelly was her maiden name and the name she always went by. Deceased has often told me as to her parents, she said she was born in Limerick - that she was 25 years of age - and from there went to Wales when very young. She told me she came to London about 4 years ago. Her father's name was John Kelly, he was a gauger at some iron works in Carnarvonshire. She told me she had one sister, who was a traveller with materials from market place to market place. She also said she had six brothers at home and one in the army, one was Henry Kelly. I never spoke to any of them. She told she had married when very young in Wales. She was married to a collier, she told me his name was Davis or Davies, I think Davies. She told me she was lawfully married to him until he died in an explosion. She said she lived with him 2 or 3 years up to his death. She told me she was married at the age of 16 years. She came to London about four years ago, after her husband's death. She said she first went to Cardiff and was in an infirmary there 8 or 9 months and followed a bad life with a cousin whilst in Cardiff. When she left Cardiff she said she came to London. In London she was first in a gay house in the West End of the town. A gentleman there asked her to go to France. She described to me she went to France. As she told me as she did not like the part she did not stay there long, she lived there about a fortnight. She did not like it and returned. She came back and lived in Ratcliffe Highway for some time, she did not tell me how long. Then she was living near Stepney Gas Works. Morganstone was the man she lived with there. She did not tell me how long she lived there. She told me that in Pennington Street she lived at one time with a Morganstone, and with Joseph Fleming, she was very fond of him. He was a mason's plasterer. He lived in Bethnal Green Road. She told me all this, but I do not know which she lived with last, Flemming used to visit her. I picked up with her in Commercial Street, Spitalfields. The first night we had a drink together and I arranged to see her the next day, and then on the Saturday we agreed to remain together and I took lodgings in George Street where I was known, George Street, Commercial Street. I lived with her from then till I left her the other day."

The first important step is to examine both accounts in detail to see if there are any internal inconsistencies or contradictions. The fact that the first statement is much briefer is not in itself surprising. We must remember the context. If, as I believe, Barnett had no part in Kelly's murder, then this deposition was made to the police on the same day as the woman with whom he had lived as de facto husband, and for whom all indications would lead us to believe he cared deeply, had been murdered in an unbelievably savage and very public manner. We would certainly expect him to be in deep shock, mingled perhaps with more than a little guilt that their recent differences and his moving out had left her alone and vulnerable. However, we must examine both of Barnett's statements in detail and see what inconsistencies - of substance or emphasis - are to be found therein. Indeed there are a number of these:

1) In his police statement, Barnett says Kelly told him "on one occasion" about her father and brother. In the version at the inquest this becomes "deceased has often told me as to her parents."

2) The police statement says John Kelly was foreman at an ironworks, whereas at the inquest he was described as a gauger.

3) In the police version the location of John Kelly (and presumably the whole family) was Carmarthen or Carnarvon, but at the inquest Barnett said it was Carnarvonshire. It may seem a small point but the "-shire" may be important. Barnett is specifying a whole county, not one town.

4) In his police statement Barnett was very specific in saying Kelly had a brother named Henry, known to his comrades as Johnto, who was serving in the 2nd Battalion Scots Guards. The inquest version is much less certain, saying that Kelly had six brothers at home and one in the army and that one of these brothers was named Henry. This second account does not make it clear that the brother serving in the army and Henry were one and the same person.

5) At the inquest Barnett, when talking of Kelly's husband, although using both variants of his name as in the police statement, states his belief that Davies was the correct version.

In order to put Barnett's outline of Kelly's life to the test in the context of existing documentary evidence we need to assemble an approximate chronology for these events.

1862 or 1863 - Kelly born in Limerick. If she were truly 25 years old at the time of the murders, the year she was born would depend on when her birthday fell. If she were born after the 9th of November, she would have become 26 years of age late in 1888, and thus would have been born in 1862. Otherwise, her year of birth would have been 1863. We must also note, as in the comment about Carnarvonshire, that saying she was born in Limerick does not specify whether she was born in the city or the county of that name.

Kelly allegedly moved to Wales when "very young." This is such a subjective term as to be impossible to interpret with any degree of certainty. To fit this into the context of available records, for Kelly to appear in the first available UK census, that of 1871, the family would have to have moved to Wales before the time that Mary Jane was seven or eight years old. This could very conceivably be within the realms of "very young". But Barnett also describes her as being "very young" when she married, to which he puts the age of 16 years. All we can say is that if Barnett's facts, or rather his reporting of them as recounted by Kelly, are correct, then Mary had been living in Wales long enough to have met and become sufficiently enamoured of the collier Davies (or had a sufficiently long dalliance to become pregnant by him if it was not a love match) by the age of sixteen, which would place us in late 1878 or 1879.

The next landmark on the road is the death of Davies. Kelly married him at sixteen, lived with him two or three years until his death which gives us the time frame for his demise as 1880 to 1882.

The Cardiff interlude lasted from the death of Davies until 1884, the year she allegedly moved to London. The only time reference Barnett quotes is the 8 or 9 months that Kelly spent in an infirmary, a period of time, perhaps, suspiciously close to that of a pregnancy carried to term. No record has ever been found of this stay of Kelly's, and we cannot be sure that it would have been in the main Cardiff Infirmary. The phrase that she "followed a bad life with a cousin," is intriguing. The usual interpretation is that the cousin of Kelly's was a prostitute and she led Mary into the life of an "unfortunate." That is certainly a possibility, but we must remember that the gender of the cousin is not specified. What if the cousin was a he, not a she? What if that stay in the infirmary was the result of a liaison with this cousin? Mere speculation, but as possible as the other version on the basis of such a paucity of fact.

In 1884 Kelly allegedly moved to London, under family circumstances that are entirely unknown. Barnett met Kelly, according to his account, around the time of Easter, 1887. During this period of, at maximum, three years, Kelly's movements and relationships were:

1) A period at the "gay house" in the West End. When Kelly first moved to London she would have been somewhere about twenty one years of

age. As we have no picture of Kelly taken in life, and the descriptions given of her range from "attractive" to "stout," we have no way of knowing just how physically alluring she was when alive. Certainly the West End brothels (as this "gay house" almost certainly was) would have attracted a very different type of both prostitute and client from the East End, so we may assume that Kelly was physically equipped, initially, to earn a reasonable living in her precarious profession. It has often been remarked that it is odd that Kelly, as a young and attractive woman, fell so quickly from the glitter of the West End to the squalor of Whitechapel. This concept may have been overplayed. The idea of Kelly as some ravishing Celtic beauty simply has no basis in the available descriptions. She is usually portrayed in the semi fictionalised accounts on film, such as "From Hell" and the 1988 version starring Michael Caine, by a suitably stunning actress. But we must remember that the descriptions of Kelly as short and stout suggest either that she was not the stunning beauty the silver screen would have us believe, or she had "let herself go" which precipitated her move to the East End sisterhood. There is also a fact about Victorian prostitution which is particularly unpalatable to modern sensibilities. Among a significant number of clients of the period, particularly those of what would be called the "better classes", there was a taste for girls of an age young enough for a modern mind to think of it as child prostitution. The simple fact is that one of the circumstances that destined Kelly to gravitate to the East End was that she had become too old for the tastes of some of the West End patrons.

2) We next have the odd episode of Kelly's alleged sojourn in France. It is usually assumed that it was about this time that Kelly first affected the use of a French rendition of her name - Marie Jeanette. Barnett uses this form of her name both in his police statement and in his inquest testimony, and it is this version which also appears on her death certificate. All other persons for whom we have police statements or inquest evidence who actually name Kelly use the form Mary Jane. As the Marie Jeanette version is on the death certificate, it is a reasonable assumption that Barnett actually registered the death and was responsible for the name being entered in this form into the register. The other occurrence of Marie Jeanette which was reported was on the engraved

plate on Kelly's coffin, but in this case it is possible that the undertaker, and the engraver who would have acted under instruction from him, would have picked up this version from the death certificate itself.

Regarding the French episode, Barnett says:

"A gentleman there asked her to go to France. She described to me she went to France. As she told me as she did not like the part she did not stay there long, she lived there about a fortnight. She did not like it and returned."

The "there" referred to in the first sentence is the "gay house" in the West End. Evidence from other sources strongly suggests that the establishment to which Kelly first moved was run by a French woman. Mrs Buki, a landlady of Kelly's prior to her meeting with Barnett, was stated by the press to have accompanied Kelly to the West End house, run by a Frenchwoman, to collect some dresses that Kelly had left there.

"This person (i.e. Mrs Buki) appears to have received Kelly direct from her West End home, for she had not been very long with her when, it is stated, both women went to the French "lady's" residence and demanded her box which contained numerous dresses of a costly description."

This same account suggests that Kelly was not above embroidering the facts to impress. The version of events that she told of her experiences is certainly at odds with what she told Barnett:

"She made no secret of the fact that while she was with the woman she drove about in a carriage and made several journeys to the French capital and in fact led a life which is described as that "of a lady.""

Kelly also blamed her life of prostitution on this French woman:

"It would appear that on her arrival in London she made the acquaintance of a French woman residing in the neighbourhood of Knightsbridge, who, she informed her friends, led her to pursue the degraded life which has now culminated in her untimely end."

Perhaps this "Madame" (in more sense than one!) had contact with expatriate Frenchmen in London and catered for their needs. It is not clear whether the "gentleman" in question was himself French but this remains a possibility. It is also not clear if the invitation to Kelly to go to France was for a holiday or on a more extended basis, as his mistress.

Whatever the circumstances, she did not stay there very long, only two weeks. The reason given is that she "did not like the part." This is ambiguous. It could mean that she did not like the part of France to which she was taken, or it could signify that she did not like the "part" or role that she was expected to play.

Two things we would most to like to know about Kelly's time in the West End establishment. How was she introduced to this gay house? Did she have any contacts in London or was she casually spotted and recruited by the Madame? And, secondly, how long did she spend in the West End? The trip to France marked, according to Barnett, the end of her West End days as, on her return to England, she moved to the Ratcliff Highway, south of Whitechapel near the docks. Sadly, the facts that would answer both these questions are now, on current knowledge, entirely beyond recall.

One consideration at this point is where the other members of Kelly's family were at this time when she moved to London. The details given by Barnett itemise her father, John Kelly, employed at an ironworks, a brother called Henry, possibly in the army, six other brothers, and a sister. Her mother, whose name is not given, remains a shadowy figure. It could be assumed that at the time of her move to London, and, indeed, at the time of her death, that the other family members, excepting the brother in the army, would still be living in Wales. However, certain statements contradict this idea. John McCarthy referred to Kelly receiving letters from Ireland. These could, of course, be from other relatives still living there, but the press statement of the unnamed City missionary who knew Kelly refers specifically to letters written to her from Ireland by her mother. Barnett says at the inquest:

"She also said she had six brothers at home and one in the army"

but it is not made clear where "at home" meant, Wales or Ireland. The logical assumption would be that the whole family came over when Kelly was young. We do not know where in the order of her siblings she came, whether these brothers and one sister were older, younger or both. It seems reasonably certain that by the time Kelly died her mother, at least, had returned to Ireland. The most likely, but unprovable, reason is that John Kelly, the father, had died and the unnamed mother had returned to the old country. Certainly in all the statements, police and inquest, and the contemporary press reports, there is no reference to Kelly's father in any terms which suggest that he was still alive.

One unresolved problem is why not one single member of Kelly's family came forward. The news and details of the murder were carried in obsessive detail, not only in the British and Irish press, but internationally. It stretches credulity to believe that all of her family members were totally oblivious to what had happened. Seven brothers, one sister, her mother, her father (if still alive) - all remained utterly mute. It could be argued that no one would want to come forward in such circumstances of ghastly murder, world headlines and lurid details of a squalid lifestyle. However, in the cases of other victims, family members came forward, identified the body, said what good they could of the deceased and laid their loved one to rest as best they could. The issue of Kelly's family's absence is complicated by the fact that there were press reports which stated that family members were on their way and would arrive in London. Where this story originated is unknown, but certainly no member of her family ever came forward, either at the time or later.

3) At this point Kelly allegedly moved into a short street which ran off St. George's Street (formerly the Ratcliff Highway) with the Mrs Buki mentioned above. After staying there for an unspecified period, Kelly allegedly took to drink and was no longer welcome.

4) Kelly moved from Mrs Buki's unknown address the short distance to Mrs Carthy (or, very probably, more correctly Mrs McCarthy) in Breezer's Hill, a short connecting road that ran south from what had been the western end of the Ratcliff Highway. There is convincing evidence that this premises, No 1 Breezer's Hill, was, if not actually a brothel, certainly run as a "safe house" for prostitutes. Three women listed at the address in the 1891 census are specifically listed as "unfortunates," i.e. prostitutes. Mrs Carthy was actually interviewed and quoted by the press. She estimates the length of time from Kelly leaving her as between eighteen months and two years. As Kelly took up with Barnett eighteen months before her death, the two year estimate would seem more credible (i.e. somewhere towards the end of 1886.) Mrs Carthy's statement is of interest in that it gives a physical description of Kelly:

"The unfortunate victim is described as being a woman about 25 years of age, 5ft 7in in height, rather stout, with blue eyes, fair complexion, and a very good head of hair. She had two false teeth in her upper jaw."

There is an odd footnote in Mrs Carthy's involvement in the Kelly story. In November 1888, Mrs Carthy related this as follows:

"Mrs. Carthy states that the deceased when she left her place went to live with a man in the building trade, and who she (Mrs. Carthy) believed would have married her. She, however, was awakened by Kelly some short time ago at two o'clock in the morning, when she was with a strange man, and asked for a bed for the night. On that occasion Mrs. Carthy asked the deceased if she was not living with the man who took her from the neighbourhood. She replied in the negative, and explained her position. From this time she was never seen in the neighbourhood."

Who this strange man was is infuriatingly intriguing as is the time at which this happened. Mrs Carthy says only "some short time ago" i.e. shortly before November 1888. This may be further proof that by the time of her death Kelly was again actively engaged in prostitution.

5) The "man in the building trade" mentioned above by Mrs Carthy seems to have been a very important person in Kelly's life. About this period of her life, Barnett has this to say:

"Then she was living near Stepney Gas Works. Morganstone was the man she lived with there. She did not tell me how long she lived there. She told me that in Pennington Street she lived at one time with a Morganstone, and with Joseph Fleming, she was very fond of him. He was a mason's plasterer. He lived in Bethnal Green Road."

This is highly confused in that two men, Morganstone and Fleming, are mentioned and three places in which they lived. In fact, she allegedly lived with Morganstone in Pennington Road and with Fleming in Bethnal Green Road. But, as we will see later, this proved not to be the case. The man named by Barnett as Morganstone has been sought under various guises. Under the name as given there is no trace, nor even under the variant Morgan Stone. Various alternatives have been suggested on the theory that Barnett would have had this information transmitted by Kelly orally and may well have misheard or misconstrued the spelling. Barnett's confusion between the similar sounding Welsh locations of

Carmarthen and Carnarvon adds some credibility to this interpretation. Variants such as Morganstern and Morganstein have been suggested, but the identity of this man is still not definitely settled.

However, with Joseph Fleming we are on firmer ground, and he is the man who seems to have had a special place in Kelly's affections. After a presumably brief stay with Morganstone, Kelly lived with Joseph Fleming, either very late in 1886 or very early 1887, if the time estimates of Mrs Carthy and Joseph Barnett are at all reliable.

Fleming was a few years older than Kelly, being born in Bethnal Green in 1859. Barnett describes him as a mason's plasterer, Mrs Carthy calls him a man in the building trade, and indeed in the 1881 census he is listed as a plasterer. This trade ran in the family, as his father, Richard Fleming, was also a plasterer. The testimony of Kelly's fondness for Fleming comes from various sources. Barnett says "she was very fond of him." Mrs Carthy says that Fleming would have married her. What the obstacle was to this, if any, is not stated. But the involvement of Kelly with Fleming goes further, in that there is evidence that she carried on seeing him after they had parted, indeed after she was living with Barnett, who says at one point in his testimony "Fleming used to visit her." The context, however, does not make it clear where or when these visits took place. Julia Venturney, of 1 Miller's Court, said:

"She told me she was very fond of another man named Joe, and he had often ill used her because she cohabited with Joe Barnett." This was in her police statement, but at the inquest she phrased her deposition as follows:

"Deceased said she was fond of another man named Joe who used to come and see her and give her money. I think he was a costermonger. She said she was very fond of him." As there was, at most, a six month period between the time Kelly left Mrs Carthy and her meeting with Joseph Barnett, during which time she had two live in relationships, it seems highly unlikely that this "Joe" of whom she was so fond could be anyone other than Joseph Fleming. If the testimony of Venturney is true, then not only did Fleming carry on visiting Kelly (presumably at Miller's Court), but he also gave her money and ill treated her because she was living with Barnett. Fleming had lived with Kelly, thought enough of her to want to marry her, carried on visiting her and giving her money when she was living with another man and abused her, probably physically, because of her relationship with Barnett, which could make him a very significant figure in the story indeed. But, as with so much to do with Kelly, there are many infuriating unknowns. If Fleming wanted to marry Kelly and she was very fond of him, what precipitated the breakdown of their relationship? For how long did Fleming continue to visit Kelly? Did Barnett know Fleming? Sadly we have no idea of Fleming's physical appearance, so we have no idea if any of the men allegedly seen in or near Miller's Court about the time of the murder could have been him. We know his age (29 at the time of the murder) but have no further physical information about him.

The whole period that we have discussed above, from the time of Kelly's arrival in London until the point when she first met Barnett, covers, at most, a total of three years, possibly less i.e. from some point in 1884 until Easter of 1887. We now reach the critical relationship of her life. The main points of their time of living together are as follows:

1) They first met in Commercial Street at Easter, 1887. They agreed almost immediately to live together, Barnett took lodgings in George Street (this road ran off Commercial Street, not the Ratcliff Highway road of the same name) where he said he was "known" and Kelly moved in with him.

2) They next moved to Little Paternoster Row, which ran off Dorset Street.

3) The couple next lived in Brick Lane.

The length of stay at all of these addresses is unknown but their final move was

4) To Miller's Court. The exact date of their tenancy is unknown. Barnett said in his police statement that he and Kelly had lived there at the time of the murder for eight months. He qualified this at the inquest as "eight months or longer." John McCarthy, the landlord, who would, presumably, be the best placed to know how long they had rented Room 13, said at the inquest "Deceased has lived in the room with Joe for ten months both together." This would place their occupancy as starting some time between January (McCarthy) and March (Barnett) of 1888.

It is ironic that this incredibly detailed inventory of Kelly's life would make it appear that we have more initial information with which to work than for any other victim. It is frustrating indeed that the exact opposite proves to be the case. The next logical step is to decide in which existing documentation Kelly should appear if all or any of the above details are true. In this context I am talking about United Kingdom records. Irish records are sadly incomplete and fragmented, many having been lost over the years. So, within the constraints of United Kingdom records, where would we expect a glimpse of Mary Jane?

1) The 1871 census - this is only a possibility in that we do not know what age Mary was when the family allegedly moved to Wales. If the age and year of birth for Kelly is correct, then at the time of this census, she would have been seven or eight years of age, again depending on when her birthday fell. If any family members were in Wales by this time we should expect them most probably to be in the counties of Carmarthen or Carnarvon. However, there is no indication of how long John Kelly stayed at the ironworks and the family may well have moved.

2) The 1881 census - this is exactly around the time when her husband, Davies, was allegedly killed in an explosion. Kelly should definitely still have been in Wales at this time, probably under the name Davies, possibly under the name Kelly if her husband had already died. Other members of her family may well still be present in Wales but we should not discount the possibility that her siblings, especially if older, had moved elsewhere.

3) The 1891 census - although Kelly herself was obviously dead by this time, and it is likely her mother, at least, had moved back to Ireland, it would be worth a search for any other family members.

4) BMD (Birth, Marriage and Death records):

a) Although Kelly herself was allegedly born in Ireland, it is not certain that she was the youngest member of the family. It is possible that some of her siblings, if younger than her, were born after the family moved to Wales.

b) The possibility of the death of her father, John Kelly, was mentioned above and should be searched for.

c) Barnett made a point of saying that Kelly and Davies were legally married, so a record of this should be sought.

d) The death of Kelly's husband in an explosion should be looked for.

5) Other records - Davies died in "an explosion." It is not specifically stated that this was a mining incident, but as he was referred to as a collier this is the most likely context. Lists of casualties in mining accidents should be consulted for the relevant period to see if there is any likely reference to Kelly's elusive husband.

In the next chapter we will see what, if anything, these records reveal in the hunt for the real Mary Kelly.

Chapter 4

The Records

Before we look at the sources of information mentioned in the last chapter, we must briefly consider under what names we might find the woman who died at Miller's Court. In the police statements and inquest testimony she is referred to by the conventional name, or permutations thereof. Some refer to her simply as "Kelly", others more familiarly as "Mary Jane." Only Barnett refers to her as Marie Jeanette Kelly, which is usually assumed to be a Francophone affectation after her visit to France. However, a number of press reports published very shortly after the murder mention two other names when referring to the woman we know as Kelly. An example of this is the following extract from the Macleod Gazette, a Canadian newspaper, published on the 11th of November, 1888:

"The name of the unfortunate woman found murdered and mutilated in her own room on Dorset street this morning is Mary Jane Lawrence. She was married to or lived with a man named Lawrence who had abandoned her."

Later in the same article we find this sentence:

"Her name is believed to have been Lizzie Fisher, but to most of the habitues of the haunts she visited she was known as Mary Jane."

So, we have two further names which occur in a sizeable number of newspaper sources - Mary Jane Lawrence and Lizzie Fisher. The number of occurrences need not necessarily be taken as giving any additional credence to these alleged names. A large number of these reports would have been syndicated, and we find large tracts of these pieces which are repeated verbatim. Of course, it would be most useful if we could identify the source and, ideally, the author of the original version of these accounts but at this remove that seems highly unlikely. The alleged Lawrence name seems founded in some kind of version of the real events in that we are told about the man Lawrence the following facts:

1) He was her husband or she had lived with him
2) He was a porter

3) He had "abandoned" her.

These features fit the relationship between Kelly and Barnett, but how his name became transmuted into Lawrence is not clear.

In the case of Lizzie Fisher, it has been suggested that there was an actual woman of that name living in the area who somehow became confused with Kelly, but again how and when this might have taken place cannot presently be explained. As these alleged names appeared very early on in the reporting of the case and before the inquest took place on the 12th of November, it seems most likely that they originated from interviews conducted by reporters in the vicinity of Spitalfields with people who knew, or claimed to know, Kelly. This would also explain why these variants appear in the press reports and not in the police or inquest papers.

The 1871 Census.

If Kelly were in the United Kingdom at this time and her life story as outlined in the last chapter has any basis in fact, we would expect her to be in Wales. As already stated, the phrase that Barnett used - that she came to Wales when "very young" - is subjective. However, if the estimate of Kelly's age at the time of her death, 25 years old, is roughly accurate, she would have been 7 or 8 years old at the time of the 1871 census. So, the rough parameters we are working to are to look for a child of approximately 7 to 8 years old and born in Ireland. Any such entry in Carmarthen or Carnarvon would be noted. Although Barnett said the family moved to Carmarthen or Carnarvon, there is no certainty that the family would have stayed there for a protracted period - owing to the nature of John Kelly's work, he may well have travelled to find employment as was common in the Victorian period.

Searching under the full given name - Mary Jane Kelly - for the Welsh census, we find only 2 entries, girls of 26 and 18, both listed as born in Wales. Using the abbreviated form of the name - Mary J. Kelly - also produces two results, aged 1 and 11, again both born in Wales. If we dispense with the middle name entirely - using just Mary Kelly - we find 69 matches. However, of these, those listed as born in Ireland reduce this number to 17 matches. Of these, only two are young girls - Mary

A Kelly aged 3 and Mary Ann Kelly aged 7. The Mary A Kelly lived in Aberdare, Glamorgan. Her parents, both Irish born, were Nicholas Kelly, a coal miner, and Joanna Kelly. No siblings are listed. The Mary Ann Kelly listed is altogether more interesting. The household details for 1871 read as follows:

Address: 48 Mumforth Street, Flint, Wales.
Head: John Kelly aged 36 born Wicklow, Ireland - Labourer
Wife: Ellen Kelly aged 30 born Dublin, Ireland
Children:
Elizabeth aged 10 born Wicklow, Ireland
Mary Ann aged 7 born Wicklow, Ireland
Patrick aged 4 born Portelley, Carnarvonshire
John aged 11 months born Flint.

This census information is intriguing. The 7 year old Mary Kelly listed here was born in Ireland but the age and place of birth of her younger brother, Patrick, shows that at some time between 1863-64 (the time of Mary's birth) and 1866-67 (the time of Patrick's birth) the family not only moved from Ireland to Wales, but specifically to Carnarvonshire, as indicated by the younger brother's place of birth. At some stage between then and April 1871 they moved to Flint where the then youngest child was born. Of course, the main objection to even a tentative identification with this young girl is her middle name - she is Mary Ann and not Mary Jane. We will meet this family again when we look at the 1881 census.

In view of the nature of census information, allowance must be made for variant spellings, so a search was made of 1871 Wales census data under the spelling of Mary Kelley. This produced four results, ranging in age from 2 to 14 years, but all were native born Welsh.

Returning to the alternative names given in a number of press articles - Lizzie Fisher and Mary Jane Lawrence - only one of these would be appropriate for a search as early as 1871. The newspaper reports that she was married to a man named Lawrence, a porter, and the census in question would obviously predate any possible marriage by many years. There is only one Lizzie Fisher listed and, although of the right age - 7 years old - she is Welsh born, as are both her parents. On the assumption that Lizzie is an abbreviation for Elizabeth, a search was made for entries under the full name of Elizabeth Fisher. There were 49 results listed but not one was born in Ireland.

The 1881 census:
According to the orthodox account of Kelly's life as related, principally, by Barnett, Kelly married at the age of 16. Thus, by the time of the 1881 census we would expect her to be married to Davis or Davies. Indeed, the census fell about the time when we would have expected the death of her husband. The chronology outlined in Barnett's account suggests Kelly was born in 1863; so if she married when she was 16, this would place this event some time around 1879. Her husband allegedly died two three years after they were married, which would take us to 1881 or 1882.

The most interesting entry in the 1871 census was the Kelly family living in Flint. This same family is listed in 1881 still living in Flint, albeit at a different address. All family members are still listed living together, including the "Mary Ann Kelly" whose age is now given as 16 years old. The full listing for 1881 is as follows:
Church Street, Flint, Wales
Head: John Kelly aged 43 born Ireland - General labourer
Wife: Ellen Kelly aged 40 born Ireland
Children:
Elizabeth aged 20 born Ireland - Domestic servant
Mary Ann aged 16 born Ireland
Patrick aged 14 born Carnarvon
John aged 11 born Flint
The one year discrepancy in Mary Ann's age (she is listed as 7 in 1871) is not at all unusual in census records - indeed many more extreme examples have been found where individuals appear to age very rapidly or to defy time! However, if the age given in 1881 is correct - 16 years old - this means at the time of the Miller's Court murder this individual would have been 23 or 24 years old, depending when in the year her birthday fell.

However, we must not at this early stage become fixated on one individual. In the Barnett account, there is no indication of either where the rest of the Kelly family were living when Mary got married - there is no certainty that they would have stayed in the Carmarthen or Carnarvon area after their initial move from Ireland - or where Mary and the mysterious Davis set up home after their marriage. The account only tells us that after her husband's death in an explosion Kelly went to live in Cardiff and spent some time in the infirmary there. So, depending on whether or not we believe the Barnett account and its chronology, by April 1881 we could be looking for Mary Kelly or Mary Davies (or Davis).

A search of the 1881 census for Wales under the full name, Mary Jane Kelly, produced only three results, all far too young and none Irish born. There were 63 "Mary Kelly" entries, of whom 19 are noted as born in Ireland. Apart from the Mary Ann Kelly living in Flint, only one other record falls within the probable age range. This individual is listed as Mary Kelly, aged 17, living at Brymbo in Denbighshire. The full household listing for this young lady is as follows:

Address: Broughton Colliery Cottages, Brymbo, Denbighshire
Head: Hubert Kelly aged 51 born Ireland - General labourer
Wife: Bridget Kelly aged 47 born Ireland
Children:
Michel (sic) aged 25 born Ireland - Labourer
John aged 24 born Ireland - General labourer
Hubert aged 19 born Ireland - General labourer
Mary aged 17 born Ireland - Servant
Patrick aged 13 born Ireland
Elizabeth aged 10 born Ireland
Garret aged 7 born Denbigh Lodge
Thomas E aged 4 born Ireland
Timothy aged 1 born Denbigh Lodge

The most interesting correlation between this family and the Barnett account is his assertion that Kelly had one sister and six or seven brothers. This Mary Kelly, indeed, had one younger sister and seven brothers. The pattern of birthplaces for the children reveals that the family moved from Ireland to Wales in time for Garret Kelly to be born in Denbigh about 1874, was back in Ireland for the birth of Thomas in about 1877 and then returned to Wales for Timothy to be born back in Denbigh in 1880. Of course, this does not necessarily mean that the whole family undertook all these trips - it was only necessary for their mother, Bridget, to be in Ireland for the birth of Thomas, for whatever reason, for this pattern to be established.

A search in 1881 under the name of Lizzie Fisher gave four results. Not only were all four too young, but three were Welsh born and one listed as born in New York. The name Elizabeth Fisher produced 56 matches, but none of these were Irish born.

We must now turn to the possibility, as in Barnett's version of events, that Kelly was already married by 1881. Looking under the name of Mary Davies, born in Ireland, produced 20 matches. Of these, only 3 were born within the timespan compatible with the Miller's Court Kelly. Of these three, in two cases Davies proved to be their birthname and the third case, the only married Mary Davies of a feasible age born in Ireland, is listed as follows:

Address: 41 North Street, Newport, Monmouthshire
Boarder:
Mary Davies aged 22 born Ireland - Married - Cheese dealer
No listing of an Irish born "Mary Davis" was found.

1891 Census:

We have two families to follow through from the 1881 census. The Kelly family living at Brymbo are listed in 1891 at a different address and the head of the household, Hubert Kelly, had died in the intervening ten years. They are listed as follows:

Address: 12 Poplar Road, Wrexham Regis, Denbighshire
Head: Bridget Kelly aged 58 born Ireland - Widow
Children:
Patrick aged 23 born Ireland - Colliery banksman

Elizabeth aged 20 born Ireland - Dressmaker
Garret F aged 17 born Denbigh - Colliery banksman
Thomas Edward aged 13 born Ireland
Timothy aged 11 born Wrexham, Denbigh
The main points of interest here are the absence of the four oldest children - Michel, John, Hubert Jnr. and Mary, and the appearance of a hitherto unlisted son, Thomas Edward, who is not mentioned in the 1881 census. By 1881, John Kelly was married to Mary E. Kelly and had set up home at Lodge, Broughton and was described as a "Top foreman - coal." Of the other three siblings I have been unable to find any trace in the census record for 1891.

Of the Flint Kelly family, listed in 1871 and 1881, there is not a trace in the Wales census of 1891. I have searched for all family members and not one could be found. The most obvious possibility was that they had all left the country, perhaps returning to Ireland. However, it was a possibility that some or all had moved to England, so the census for that country had to be searched also. Accordingly I searched for all family members - both parents and four children - but was unable to find a record of any of them. Of course, it is possible, as in the case of Hubert Kelly in the other household we looked at, that some had died. We will look at that possibility when we come to examine the births, marriages and death registers for this period.

With regard to the Lawrence and Fisher names quoted in newspaper accounts, it would seem superfluous to search for someone who by 1891 was already dead. But just as a check I searched the England and Wales censuses for 1891 for a Mary Jane Lawrence born in Ireland. There were none. Four entries were listed for an Elizabeth Fisher born in Ireland but none had a demonstrable link to London, although there were two women by the name of Elizabeth Fisher living in Shoreditch in 1891. The first was married to a German porter named John Fisher and they had a 9 year old daughter named Lizzie G. Fisher. This Elizabeth was 38 years old and born in Spitalfields. The other was a 37 year old machinist who boarded at 42 Ivy Lane, Hoxton.

Births, Marriages and Deaths:

The registers of births, marriages and deaths in the United Kingdom date back to 1837, the year Queen Victoria came to the throne. It was in that year that it first became a national requirement for all such events to be duly and properly registered and a centralised record kept. Before that date, of course, such happenings were noted but this was done on a local parish basis. This date of 1837 is very well known to anyone trying to trace their own family, as any record they need before this watershed needs to be found in the records of the church where it was registered, a much more complex process requiring a lot of delving and more than a little luck.

As things stand, there is only one event in the life of the woman who died in Miller's Court of which there is an indubitable record, and that is her death. In the index she is listed as Marie Jeanette Kelly or Davies aged about 25 and the death was registered in the last quarter of 1888 in Whitechapel - the full reference being Volume 1c page 211. Before we delve too deeply into the world of BMD (the usual abbreviation of Births, Marriages and Deaths), it would be worthwhile to explain a little as to how the available records are structured. The indices I will be repeatedly mentioning do not give full details of the events. They are compilations of the main details of the certificate issued for that type of event. Records are arranged as follows:- obviously separate indices are kept for each type - birth, marriage and death - and these entries by type are compiled quarterly each year. There will one volume for January to March, one for April to June, one for July to September and the last will cover October to December. Within each quarter entries of the relevant type will be arranged in strict alphabetical order. However, useful though they are, the index for each quarter contains very limited information. For each certificate issued the index will list the surname and forenames of the person in question, the district in which that certificate was issued and finally the volume and page number of the records for that district in which the certificate can be found. In the case of death certificates, the index also lists the age of the deceased at the time of death. Full details - such as cause of death, address of the deceased at the time of death, etc., can only be found by obtaining the full certificate.

The full details as listed on Kelly's death certificate are as follows:
Registration District: Whitechapel
Death in the Sub District of Spitalfields in County of Middlesex
When and where died: 9th November 1888 1 Miller's Court, Christchurch
Name and surname: Marie Jeanette Kelly otherwise Davies
Sex: Female
Age: about 25 years
Occupation: Prostitute
Cause of death: Severance of right carotid artery. Wilful murder against some person or persons unknown. Violent.
Signature, description and residence of informant: Certificate received from R. Macdonald, Coroner for Middlesex. Inquest held 12th November.
When registered: 17th November 1888
Signature of registrar: W. Edwards.

There are certain points of interest in the details given in the death certificate. As previously mentioned, the form of Kelly's name is the French form which it has been surmised Kelly adopted after her trip to France. This style of her name was only used by Barnett at the inquest, all other witnesses who referred to her forenames calling her Mary or Mary Jane. But if the form of her name on the certificate would have met with Barnett's approval, he surely cannot have been pleased with her description as a prostitute. The other four generally accepted victims of the Whitechapel murderer are described on their death certificates, under occupation, as follows:
Mary Nichols: "Wife of William Nichols, printing machinist. Lodging house 35 Dorset Street, Spitalfields."
Annie Chapman: "Widow of John Chapman, a coachman."
Elizabeth Stride: "Widow of John Thomas Stride, carpenter."
Catherine Eddowes: "Supposed single woman."
In the cases of all the other victims, the column of "Occupation" is completed in terms of their past or present marital status. Uniquely

Kelly is identified as a prostitute, although the question of whether the other victims were working on the streets was certainly raised at their inquests. Two facts would suggest a reason why Kelly is identified in this way when the other victims were not. The vagueness of Barnett's testimony about Kelly's former marriage did not allow her former spouse to be confirmed, and thus for her to be identified on a legal document as his widow. Also, Barnett specifically stated in his inquest testimony both that Kelly was working as a prostitute shortly before her death, and had earned her living in this way before Barnett met her.

It seems surprising that any doctor could determine among the shambles that was found at Miller's Court that the wound which actually caused death was the severance of the right carotid artery. In only one other victim, Eddowes, does the death certificate specify the direction of the fatal blow: in her case the entry reads: "Haemorrhage from the left carotid artery..." The other three victims have the following causes of death listed:

Nichols - "Syncope from loss of blood from wounds in neck and abdomen"

Chapman - "Injuries to throat and abdomen by a sharp instrument"

Stride - "Haemorrhage from severance of blood vessels in the neck"

It does seem remarkable that the death certificate of Kelly can be so specific given the gross and extensive nature of the mutilations on the body as it was found in Miller's Court. The other death certificates show that such a degree of specificity was not required to fulfil the legal definition of a cause of death, so it would be most interesting to know on what basis the severance of the right carotid artery was arrived at as the fatal blow.

Virtually all sources agree that Kelly was Irish by birth. There is one unnamed source, an alleged acquaintance of Kelly, quoted in some press accounts who not only said that Kelly was a "Welshwoman" but that she spoke fluent Welsh. Of course, these two statements are not necessarily mutually exclusive. The Welsh language, especially in rural areas, would have been more extensively spoken than it is today and if Kelly came, or rather was taken by the family to Wales, when a very young child, it is not at all unlikely that she would have acquired at least a working knowledge of the language. The other possibility is that Kelly actually spoke Erse, i.e. Gaelic Irish, which, to an untutored ear, could conceivably be mistaken for Welsh. However, as previously stated, the search of Irish records for Kelly's birth has not provided a definitive sighting of her. Sadly, in certain areas, due to the vagaries of history and the loss of documentation, Irish records are far from complete. The record has been found of a Mary Kelly born in Limerick in 1863 but this has not been universally accepted as relating to the Miller's Court victim.

When we are looking at BMD records, we would appear on the firmest ground when it comes to Mary Kelly's early marriage. Barnett's account tells us four things which should make this relatively easy to track down:
1) He specifically says Kelly was her maiden name
2) She married when she was 16
3) He stresses that she was legally married
4) The man she married was named Davis or Davies - Barnett in his inquest statement favoured the latter.
This would imply a marriage some time around 1879. Also, we can reasonably infer that the marriage took place in Wales, but we cannot restrict ourselves to looking in the two mentioned locations - Carmarthen or Carnarvon. This is for two reasons. If the family moved to either location when Mary was very young, it was more than probable that they could have moved on to another location by the time of her marriage. Also, it is possible that the groom, Davies, came from elsewhere in Wales and they actually married in his home parish.

An initial search of the marriage index was carried out allowing a two year margin either side of the target year, 1879. Firstly I looked for any marriage of a Mary Kelly which took place in Wales. The result of this search were as follows:
1877 - No results
1878 - One result. This marriage took place in Merthyr Tydfil in the 2nd quarter of that year between Mary Kelly and either William Flynn

or William Wigley.

(A note here on the marriage indices - this lists all persons on each register page without specifying which individuals married each other. This can only be verified by obtaining the full certificate, which would be done if the index provides sufficient indication that this may be the marriage which is being sought.)

1879 - Only one Welsh marriage is listed. In the last quarter of that year a Cecilia Mary Kelly was married in St Asaph, Flintshire to a William Jones. In that same year there were two marriages of a female named Mary Jane Kelly, but both of these took place in Lancashire. The first of these married Michael Fairhurst or Jeffrey Hart, and the second was wed to Frederick Beatty or William Leigh.

1880: The following Welsh marriages were found:

a) In Crickhowell, Breconshire, in the third quarter of the year, Mary Kelly married John Crowley.

b) In Atcham, Montgomeryshire, in the third quarter, Mary Kelly married Thomas Dolman or John Jones.

c) In the first quarter the marriage took place at Neath, Glamorgan between Mary Jane Kelly and either John Morgan or William Williams.

d) In the third quarter, at Newport, Monmouth, Mary Jane Kelly was married to Richard Rees or Edward Wilkes.

1881 - no records were found.

Mr. Davies or Davis is noticeable by his absence! In fact during this whole five year period (1877-1881) I have so far only found one record anywhere of a Mary Kelly marrying a man named Davis or Davies. This took place in Shoreditch in the first quarter of 1881 and involved a Mary Ann Kelly and a John Brook Davis. Fuller details of this marriage are given below.

So what are we to make of this absence of a record that seems the most promising lead from Barnett's testimony? Well, logically there are only a limited number of possibilities.

1) The real name of the woman who died at Miller's Court was not Mary Jane Kelly

2) If her name was Kelly she did not marry a man named Davies or any variant thereof

3) Kelly and Davies were not actually married

4) If they did marry, this wedding, for whatever reason, took place outside Wales.

The most readily accessible of these possibilities to check is that the couple married outside Wales. We will look at the same span of years (1877 to 1881) but this time at the English rather than the Welsh records. As the number of matches could reasonably be expected to be much higher, we will initially specifically look for a Mary Jane Kelly as opposed to just a Mary Kelly. The results of this search were as follows:

1877: Two marriages are registered for Mary Jane Kelly, one in Tynemouth and one in Manchester. Neither involved a Davies.

1878: Five marriages were listed - one in County Durham, two in Devon, one in Lancashire and one on the Isle of Wight. Again, no Davies is listed for any of these events.

1879: Two marriages, both in Lancashire, were found. No Davies entry was in evidence.

1880: Two marriages were found, both in Devon. Neither lady married a Davies.

1881: Three marriages are registered, two in Lancashire and one in Yorkshire. No Davies was involved.

When we broaden the search to look for any marriage involving a partner named Mary Kelly outside of Wales, we find the following results:

1877 - 37 records found, none involving a Davies

1878 - 39 matches, no Davies listed

1879 - 36 matches, no Davies listed

1880 - 40 matches, no Davies listed

1881 - 32 matches, one match on Davis.

The 1881 marriage is the wedding between Mary Ann Kelly and John Brook Davis registered in Shoreditch in the first quarter of that year. As this is the only marriage so far found between a Mary Kelly and a partner named Davis, it is important to follow this up and see if anything further can be found. There is only one census entry specifically under the named of John Brook Davis which occurs in the 1871 records. He is listed as a 19 year old unmarried boarder at 59 Township, Worcester and his occupation is listed as a chemist's assistant. Interestingly, he is listed as Welsh born, specifically as coming from Rhyl, Flintshire. He lodged with his employer, a chemist named Edwin Timms, aged 42. There is also another record of a marriage in Islington in 1883 between a John Brook Davis and either Eliza Faulkner or Charlotte King. However, it would appear that the Worcester, Welsh born John Davis is unrelated to the couple who married in Shoreditch in 1881. What I believe is their household record is listed in the 1881 census as follows:

Address: 33 Fanshaw Street, London
Head: John B Davis aged 23 born Shoreditch - Picture frame maker
Wife: Mary A Davis aged 18 born Bethnal Green - Boot machinist.

What of the interesting looking family from Flint we found in the 1871 and 1881 census information? There were four siblings, of which the younger, the sons Patrick and John, are listed as born in Wales. In the 1871 census we are told that at the time of the enumeration (i.e. April 1871) John Kelly was aged 11 months and born in Flint. This means we can date the birth with unusual precision to May 1870. And indeed we do find the birth registered at Holywell (a few miles from Flint) in the second quarter of 1870 (Volume 11b Page 294). The older brother, Patrick, is listed in 1871 as 4 and in 1881 as 14, and born in Carnarvon. This means, depending on when his birthday fell, he was born either in 1866 or 1867. In fact, no trace of the birth of a Patrick Kelly registered in or near Carnarvon can be found between 1864 and 1868. As already stated, the fate of John Kelly, father of the Flint household, is unknown. Although we have two ages given for John - 36 in 1871 and 43 in 1881 - the subsequent unknown place of residence of the family makes any definite identification as to his date of death impossible. Other records we might hope to find in the BMD records - such as the marriage of Elizabeth Kelly - simply are not there as far as can be traced. The whole family, including Mary Ann Kelly, simply disappear. In the standard account of Mary Jane Kelly's life, no mention is made of her father, John Kelly, after the alleged move of the family to Wales. However, there are mentions that by the time of the murder Mary Jane's mother, widowed or otherwise, had returned to Ireland and was in correspondence with her daughter in London. John McCarthy made mention of mail that Kelly received from Ireland and, more specifically, the unnamed City missionary who was interviewed by a reporter claimed that he had seen letters from Kelly's mother which she had received. It has been suggested that this showing of personal correspondence to the missionary, coupled with Barnett's testimony that he read aloud to Kelly from the newspapers, is evidence of illiteracy on the part of Kelly, but this cannot be proven and, even it if it were so, it would not be that great a surprise for someone of Kelly's background and upbringing.

The last documentary source we must look at relates to the death of Kelly's alleged husband, Davis or Davies. Barnett testified that Kelly married when 16 - somewhere about 1879 - that she was married for two or three years when her husband was killed in "an explosion." As Davies is referred to by Barnett as a collier, i.e. a coalminer, it is usually assumed that this was in some kind of pit disaster. This is not absolutely certain, but the balance of probability suggests that it was very likely the case. This explosion, if associated with the colliery and his place of work, could have taken one of two forms. If it was an underground explosion, the most likely cause would have been the ignition of flammable gas. However, there was certainly a history of pithead incidents and disasters involving the explosion of pumping or winding machinery. In the early 1880s, the period we are looking at in this context, there would certainly still have been a significant use of steam powered winding and pumping gear at the pithead, so it is certainly not improbable that if Davies did die in an explosion, it may not necessarily have been an incident underground.

So, we are looking for a Welsh mining disaster in 1881 or 1882 whose victims included a DAVIES or DAVIS. In fact 1881 was notable in the lack of fatalities for that year. In 1882 there were two incidents that resulted in fatalities:
On January 15th 1882, at Risca pit 4 died

On February 11th 1882, at Coedcae pit, 6 died.
On March 3rd 1882 at Henwaen Blaina, 5 died.
The death roll for the Coedcae incident on February 11th is:
George Warlow
Thomas Williams
Jacob Thomas
Howell James Lewis
Benjamin James
Joseph Rowlands
The Henwaen Blaina incident is described thus:
"On 3rd March 1882, five men were killed in a localised explosion. It was reported that their bodies had been blown a considerable distance."
A photograph exists of the workforce before this explosion
The death roll was:
William Bennet aged 26
? Hawkins aged 65
? Jones aged 42
John Jones aged 48
Thomas Miles aged 25
I have been unable to locate a list of the fatalities for the Risca incident of 15th January 1882.

There is one incident which occurred on December 10th 1880 and so impinges very closely on the possible time frame we are looking at. This disaster occurred at the Naval Steam Colliery, Penygraig and resulted in 96 deaths. From the death roll the following names and details are taken:
Evan Davies aged 49 from Coedymeibion, married with 4 children
Evan Davies, no details
John Davies, aged 42 from Penygraig, married with 2 children
John Davies, no details
John Davies, no details
William Davies from Ffwrdamos
William R Davies aged 23 from Penygraig
The deaths were registered in the January-March quarter of 1881

under the district of Pontypridd.
Evan Davies aged 49
Evan Davies aged 32
John Davies aged 42
John Davies, no details
William R Davies aged 23 (his middle name is Roderick)
William Davies, no details.
None of these victims of the name of Davies or Davis can be linked in legal marriage to a Mary Kelly.

So, what does all this documentation tell us, if anything? Well, we must admit from the outset that there is no firm, unequivocal sighting which fits the Miller's Court victim in all respects. Of the cases some seem worthy of interest. There is only one case on record of a marriage between a Mary Kelly and a man named Davis, in this case John Brook Davis. However, this occurred in Shoreditch in 1881 and so contradicts the Barnett story in many respects, but principally in his assertion that Kelly did not move to London until 1884. The Flintshire Kelly family is interesting in that it fulfils some, but by no means all, the criteria raised by Barnett's story, namely:

1) The head of the family is named John Kelly
2) The family includes a daughter named Mary Kelly born in Ireland circa 1864
3) Both parents were Irish born
4) The family would have moved from Ireland to Wales some time before 1867 to Carnarvon, where their son Patrick Kelly was born
5) Mary Kelly had one sister, Elizabeth
6) All trace of the family from the 1891 census, in both England and Wales, is currently undiscovered.

However, it must be said that the Flintshire family differ in significant respects from the conventional account of the Miller's Court Kelly:

1) The daughter of the Flintshire family is Mary Ann not Mary Jane
2) She had one sister but only two brothers, not the six or seven mentioned by Barnett
3) The head, John Kelly, is listed only as a general labourer, not specifically as working in an ironworks. However, the first mention we

see is in 1871 which is at least four years after the family moved to Wales. A change of occupation is not that unlikely.

4) The birthplaces mentioned for this family in 1871 are in the Wicklow and Dublin areas, to the east of Ireland. Limerick, where Mary Jane Kelly was allegedly born, is in the south west of Ireland.

Chapter 5

The Mysteries of Miller's Court

There are certain aspects of the Miller's Court murder which are, or have been made into, nagging mysteries. The minutiae of what was or was not found in the room after Kelly's corpse was discovered have been endlessly discussed, teased apart and invested with layers of meaning. In this context I am talking only about alleged features of the crime scene itself, not apparent contradictions such as sightings of Kelly after logic dictated that she was already dead. These other aspects will be looked at later.

The order of events at the crime scene, as we saw earlier, was that, after the initial flurry of activity which followed Bowyer and McCarthy summoning the police shortly after 10.45. a.m., there was a period of enforced and, surely, frustrating inactivity caused by the confusion and uncertainty over the possible arrival and use of bloodhounds. Eventually the room at Miller's Court was broken into at about 1.30 p.m. and the medical men then spent up to four hours in their examination of the remains before they were removed to Shoreditch Mortuary. Considering the small size of the room (only approximately twelve feet square) and the fact that a posse of medical men was cited as being present at the scene, it can surely only have been after the remains were removed that Abberline had a free hand to investigate the room and examine its contents. The most discussed of the mysteries attendant upon the crime scene were:

1) The locked door and the missing key
2) The clothing found in the room
3) The fire lit in the room
4) The writing on the wall.

There is much confusion on the matter of the locked door and the missing key. One point must be made plain straightaway. Sources at the time make it clear that the door which led into Kelly's room from the passageway into Miller's Court was opened by means of a latch key. A latch lock, as opposed to the more secure lever lock, was simply a metal bar or bolt on the inside of the door which fitted into a small metal plate located on the door jamb to keep it closed. The latch key was essentially a simple metal lever which could be used through the keyhole to raise the metal latch from the outside to enable the door to be opened from without. Two of the main features of a latch lock are that the door can be closed on exiting without using a key as the latch will simply fall into place as the door is closed, and the door can be opened from inside without the need for a key by manually raising the latch. References to the door being locked and the lack of a key are mostly from press accounts of the time and these are of interest in trying to settle the question of whether the key was lost, if so when, or whether the killer may have taken the key with him.

The Daily Telegraph of 10 November : "The last person to have left the place must have closed the door behind him, taking with him the key from the spring lock, as it is missing." The spring lock referred to here is a variant of the latch lock in which the latch is kept in place when the door is closed by a spring rather than just by gravity.

The Daily News of 10 November: "The lock of the door was a spring one, and the murderer apparently took the key away with him when he left, as it cannot be found."

The East London Advertiser of 17 November: "On looking through the keyhole he (Bowyer) found the key was missing."

The Star of 10 November: "He (Bowyer) then tried the handle of the door and found it was locked. On looking through the keyhole he found the key was missing."

The Times contains substantially a compilation of the above phrases, virtually verbatim, but adds, with regard to an alleged sighting of Kelly with a man about midnight, "The pair reached Miller's Court about midnight, but they were not seen to enter the house. The street door was closed, but the woman had a latchkey, and, as she must have been fairly sober, she and her companion would have been able to enter the house and enter the woman's room without making a noise."

These press reports lay the seeds of all the later variants and speculations of what actually happened to the key - that the killer had the key prior to the murder, that the killer took the key with him and so on. In contrast to these press reports are the police statements and inquest testimony. Neither Bowyer not McCarthy made any reference to looking through the keyhole, but only to knocking on the door and then going round and looking in through the broken window. In fact, the only reference to the key in the police or inquest evidence comes from Inspector Abberline, who said at the inquest: "I am informed by the witness Barnett that the key had been missing for some time and that they opened the door by reaching round through the window."

Another variance of fact is the time at which the police, specifically Superintendent Arnold, finally ordered the door of Kelly's room to be broken in to allow access to the murder scene. The press reports frequently report that this happened shortly after the discovery of the body at 10.45. The Daily Telegraph, for example, says: "Nothing, however, was done until the arrival of Mr. T. Arnold, the Superintendent of the H Division of Metropolitan Police, who, shortly after eleven o'clock, gave orders for the door of the room to be broken open." However, Dr. Phillips at the inquest testified as follows: "I remained until about 1.30 when the door was broken open I think by Mr. McCarthy - I think by direction of Superintendent Arnold who had arrived." It would seem that the testimony under oath of the police divisional surgeon, who had been kept waiting at the scene of the crime for two and a quarter hours, is more likely correct. Indeed, Phillips's testimony shows in his stated time of arrival at the crime scene that the time quoted in the press was nonsensical. Phillips says "I was called by the police about 11 o'clock and proceeded to Millers Court which I entered at 11.15 a.m." According to the press account the door had already been opened by this time, but this was patently not the case.

The whole point of the above comparison of the press and inquest accounts is how quickly and how comprehensively misinformation and plain error could creep into the written accounts of the murder. With so many press reports being syndicated and plagiarised, these errors spawned like mushrooms in the dark. So, in considering the matter of the missing key, we must bear in mind that no mention whatever was made in police statements or at the inquest of Bowyer peering through the keyhole and noticing that the key was missing. And the certainty of the assertion that "the woman had a latch key" in The Times is flatly contradicted by their own words in the same sentence that "they (Kelly and the man) were not seen to enter the house." If they were not seen to enter, how could the observer know that Kelly opened the door with a key and not, as Abberline reported, manually via the window? The whole matter of the key and the locked door is dealt with at the inquest in one matter of fact, almost dismissive sentence of Abberline's - that the key had been lost and the door opened via the broken window. I can see no firm grounds for doubting the simplicity of Abberline's statement or for embellishing the facts into the murderer surreptitiously making off with the key. In my opinion, the simple statement of the key's loss is the most likely explanation, and almost certainly what actually happened.

The matter of the clothing found in the room at Miller's Court devolves into three questions:
1) What happened to Kelly's clothing?
2) What other clothing was in the room?
3) What clothing was burned in the fire?
In his inquest testimony, Dr. Phillips said "she had only her under linen garment on her." This seems plain enough, but Dr. Thomas Bond's post mortem report begins in the following way: "the body was lying naked in the middle of the bed." This apparent contradiction is usually resolved by reference to the larger of the two post mortem photographs of Kelly. It is argued that this clearly shows her to be wearing some sort of linen chemise but a close examination of the conformation of these areas of cloth show this may not be the case. In the photograph, the two main areas where this "garment" is visible are over Kelly's left shoulder and draped over the top of her left thigh and across the lower part of the abdominal cavity. However, close scrutiny of these areas shows that the portion over the left shoulder is simply pulled or laid over this area, and shows no similarity to the sleeve of a chemise. Indeed the pale material continues under the left arm and joins up with the cloth laid over the top of the thigh. The whole conformation looks much more like a section of a sheet or a pillow case which has been pulled up round sections of the body rather than any kind of undergarment. Of course, Kelly was

dressed when she last went out on the evening of the 8th, or the early hours of the 9th of November. Whether she stripped, or was stripped, prior to what she believed would be a normal client, or whether the body was stripped by the killer prior to his carrying out the mutilations, will never be known. Various press accounts report that Kelly's clothing was not only accounted for but appeared to have been neatly stowed away. The Daily Telegraph has this to say: "That the woman had had no struggle with her betrayer was shown by her position and the way in which her garments, including a velvet bodice, were arranged by the fireplace." Two of the witnesses described what Kelly was wearing when they last saw her. Mary Ann Cox, in her police statement, said she saw Kelly at a quarter to midnight on the 8th November, at which time she was wearing "a linsey frock, red knitted crossover around shoulder, had no hat or bonnet on." In her inquest testimony, the time of the sighting was cited as midnight, and her garments were described as "no hat on, she a red pellorine and a dark shabby skirt." A pellorine, more properly spelled pelerine, is defined as "A woman's cape, usually short, with points in front." The name comes from the French word meaning a female pilgrim, and presumably refers to the traditional pilgrim's cloak. The other witness who described what Kelly was wearing was Caroline Maxwell, who claimed to have seen Kelly at 8.30 on the morning of the 9th November. We will discuss the anomalous timing of this testimony later, but in the present context, we must note that in her police statement, Mrs Maxwell said Kelly was wearing "a dark dress black velvet body, and coloured wrapper round her neck." In her inquest deposition, the apparel of Kelly was described as "a dark skirt - velvet body - and morone shawl and no hat." The "morone" (i.e. maroon) shawl may well be the same garment as the red knitted crossover and red pellorine, but the reference to a "velvet body" (i.e. velvet bodice) is most interesting as this is the only garment of Kelly's specifically mentioned in the account of her clothing found in the room.

There was reference to other clothing left in the room by Maria Harvey, who had slept in the room at Miller's Court with Kelly on the Monday and Tuesday of the week of the murder. Harvey was a laundress and in both her police and inquest evidence gave a detailed list of articles of clothing she had left in Kelly's room, and which would still have been there at the time of the murder. These are itemised as: -

2 men's shirts

1 boy's shirt

A man's black overcoat

A black crepe bonnet with black strings

A child's white petticoat

Of these items which were present at the time of the murder, Harvey stated that only the man's overcoat had been shown to her by the police. We hear no more of the fate of the rest of these garments.

We now come to the much debated subject of the fire that was lit in the room at Miller's Court. At the inquest the only mention of this was by Inspector Abberline who had this to say: "There had been a large fire, so large as to melt the spout off the kettle. I have since gone through the ashes in the grate and found nothing of consequence except that articles of woman's clothing had been burnt which I presume was for the purpose of light as there was only one piece of candle in the room." At this moment we are only looking at the issue of clothing burned in the grate - we will look at other issues raised by the fire shortly. The press accounts which refer to the fire in the room confirm that the ashes were examined - in fact, some say they were passed through a sieve - and that nothing of importance was found. Some press accounts add the fact that part of the wire rim of a woman's bonnet was found in the ashes. The questions that arise at this point are - what clothing was burnt and why? One unanswered - and unanswerable - question is whether there was a fire already going in the grate at 13 Miller's Court when the killer, by whatever means, gained entry. It seems likely to me on two counts that this would have been the case. In view of the time of year it would not be at all unlikely that Kelly would have had a fire burning. And it seems most unlikely that the killer would pause during or after the mutilations to Kelly's body to light a fire from scratch to burn articles of clothing for whatever purpose. But of course this begs the question of who actually burned the clothing. It is usually assumed by most observers - including Abberline - that the killer himself burned the clothes. As to what clothing was burned, various exotic theories have emerged to explain this strange act. One frequently quoted is that the killer burnt part of his own clothing, which was bloodstained, to avoid venturing out into the street in such a condition. This seems to me most unlikely. Unless it was a lighter inner garment, such as a shirt, a man's outer garment, especially a winter garment, of the period would most likely have been of a fairly dense material such as tweed or serge. Such a garment, especially if blood soaked to the extent that the killer felt he had to destroy it, would simply not burn but would at most smoulder, and substantial amounts of it would surely have remained to be found by Abberline. Another theory is that the killer burnt part of Kelly's clothing. But if this were done to destroy evidence - the most conceivable motive - this is nonsensical in the light of the horrifically mutilated body left on the bed to be discovered. The most likely answer seems to be apparent - that the clothing burned in the grate at Miller's Court was the clothing left by Maria Harvey, except for the man's overcoat for the very reason mentioned above - that such a heavy, dense material would not burn but merely smoulder in a small, domestic grate. But how do we equate this with Abberline's statement that he found the remains of a woman's clothing? All the available statements, and the stated ferocity of the fire, suggest that all Abberline found were ashes, which would be impossible to identify with certainty as male or female clothing. The only item which would not burn and would be left in a recognisable form was the wire rim of the crepe bonnet left by Maria Harvey.

This brings us on to more general questions about the fire, such as the melting of the kettle and the purpose for which such a fire was lit. Abberline described it as "a large fire" - but it not clear whether he meant large as in size, with much material burned, or large as in temperature, for the main result of this largeness is the melting of the kettle. But again these assertions beg many questions. How can we be sure that all of the material that was found by Abberline was the result of a single fire burned on the night of 8th to 9th November? Is it not possible that what Abberline found was the accumulation of ashes from a few or even many days' fires? Are we to assume that Kelly was punctilious enough to clean out the grate every day and that, therefore, all the debris found on the day of the murder was the product of only one large fire instead of days of small fires? All the mysteries regarding the fire are based on the assumption that it was the killer who burned the clothing and that everything that was found in the grate that day resulted from one conflagration. We do not know what type or quantity of fuel Kelly had in her room - wood or coal - but if she took a client back to her room on the evening of the 8th and the room was dark and cold, it is not inconceivable that Kelly herself stoked up the fire with all she had to hand, the more easily burned articles left by Maria Harvey. Again we have no way of knowing for certain that the melting of the kettle actually happened on the night of the murder. If it had happened earlier it is hardly the sort of circumstance that a visitor would have commented on or even noticed - it is an event small in itself, which only became important because of its location and its assumed synchronicity with the murder. One note about the melted kettle, which all revolves around one word. Abberline did not say that the fire had melted the spout "of" the kettle - he said it had melted the spout "off" the kettle. This would only make sense in one context. The type of kettle used by someone of Kelly's means, which were limited to say the least, would in all likelihood have been a cheap tin kettle in which the spout was soldered to the body of the object. The melting point of tin is 232 degrees Celsius, 450 degrees Fahrenheit - a rather high temperature for a small domestic fire, however well stoked. However the melting point of solder, specially the type of low grade solder used in cheap tin ware, is somewhere about 118 degrees Celsius, i.e. only 18 degrees above the boiling point of water and certainly achievable in a domestic grate. What I suggest may have happened and what Abberline implied in his statement, was that the heat of the fire, either on the night of the murder or some previous occasion, weakened or even melted the solder joint on the kettle and the spout fell off.

We now come to one of the most recently alleged and most fiercely debated mysteries of the room in which Mary Kelly died. In 1992 there came to the attention of the publishing world the document which has become generally known as the "Ripper Diary". It was not long before this curious piece of writing came to the world's attention and it has been generating much heat and partisan debate ever since. This is such a complex topic with so many subsequent ramifications that I do not have time or space to go into all aspects of it here. Nor, indeed, is this the place to do so as it fully deserves a detailed treatment in its own right. All that concerns me at present is the assertion that the killer left two initials on the wall behind the bed and that not only do these give a clue to who the killer was but even point to his motive. The text of the Diary is not laid out in the format of a traditional journal with convenient dates and clear time divisions. The narrative is disjointed and the only unequivocal date mentioned in the work is that at the end where the diary is signed - the date given being the 3rd of May, 1889. Although the hand that penned the Diary, whoever it was, never mentions James Maybrick by name I think there can be no doubt, whatever one's feelings about the real author or date of the work, that the reader is intended to believe that Maybrick was the writer. Maybrick himself died on 11th of May 1889, eight days after the alleged date of the last entry in the Diary. Although, as already stated, no entry in the Diary is dated, some of the principal events described can be clearly identified - for the purposes of the current work we are, of course, looking for the Diary references to Kelly. The murder is described on pages 241 to 245 of the document, and there are two references to the so called "writing on the wall." Both references are, as is the nature of the diary, oblique and quasi cryptic. The first comes in the doggerel verse, typical of that which fills much of the Diary:

"An initial here and a initial there
Would tell of the whoring mother."

It does seems odd that the author would in the space of one line get the indefinite article both right and wrong - even though the author does quote the passage correctly a few lines further on. But we are not concerned here with his literary style or his grammatical correctness, only with the alleged content as it applies to Kelly. The second mention in the same section of the Diary says:

"I left it there for the fools but they will never find it. I was too clever. Left it in front for all eyes to see. That amuses me."

The now accepted explanation of these passages is that the killer - in this scenario, Maybrick - left two initials written in blood and visible on the back wall of the room in Miller's Court. These letters can allegedly be seen on the wall immediately above the angle of the wrist of Kelly's left hand which lays across her stomach. The two initials that Maybrick wrote are, allegedly, "F M." These are the initials of his wife, Florence Maybrick, who was eventually charged with his murder by poisoning, convicted, sentenced to death but eventually imprisoned. The whole rationale of the Diary (if such a word can be used of a document which is, or deliberately sets out to be, steeped in insanity) is that the killer, Maybrick, committed the murders as a result of his wife's infidelity with Alfred Brierly. Florence is repeatedly referred to in the Diary as the "whore" or the "whoring mother" and Brierly as the "whore master." So the writer of the Diary - Maybrick or whoever - is gloating in his intellectual superiority over the "fools" who do not see the clue in front of their very eyes, the initials of the woman, the whore, whose perfidious behaviour has given rise to all these insane, unspeakable events. At least, that is the writer's version of things.

As is common in the field of Ripper studies, the reality is both more complex and less clear cut. The writer says he left the initials "in front for all eyes to see" but it has to be said that even when the location of the alleged initials is pointed out, there are many people who are simply unable to see them. It reminds me of those computer generated 3D pictures that were in vogue some years ago - some could see the depth effect instantly, some were never able to achieve it. In this context it is important to bear in mind that the larger photograph we have of Kelly's remains lying on the bed is not at all clear, the image being in many respects degraded with numerous miscellaneous marks upon the image which cannot be definitively interpreted. This kind of image is very fertile ground for the human brain's propensity not only to see patterns where none exist but to actively impose structure and order on disconnected stimuli. This is analogous to our seeing shapes in the stars and naming them as constellations, or seeing shadows in the dark as faces or human figures. Our brains desperately strive to make sense out of chaos, order out of random images. We have no control over this propensity - it is the way we are programmed and in evolutionary terms it has served us very well. Personally, I can sort of see the M but the F of the alleged initials eludes me. Whether these shapes are random marks on the photograph or wall, perhaps even marks of blood, will probably never be known.

One other observation which I have never seen mentioned elsewhere seems to me important. In the comment - ""I left it there for the fools but they will never find it. I was too clever. Left it in front for all eyes to see" - who are the fools the writer is referring to? The police? Is it a battle of wills between the police and the killer, who is showing his imagined cleverness and superiority by leaving what he obviously sees as a blatant clue? But why then does he say it was left for "all eyes" to see? That he was leaving it for posterity? But that does not make sense as it relies on two circumstances coming about which the killer at the time of the murder could not possibly have known. The tone of the Diary suggests that these entries relating to the killings were made within a short time of the act itself when the mood of elation and superiority was still upon him, while the rush of what he had done still excited him. The preamble to the entry interpreted as relating to the Kelly murder starts with the words "I have read about my latest." The first press coverage of the killing - which of course includes no mention of the initials on the wall - made the papers late on the 9th November, with much fuller coverage the following day. This suggests the killer is trying to give us the impression he is recollecting the Kelly murder within a day or two of the deed. But in order for him to leave the initials on the wall for "all eyes to see" - i.e. to be spotted latter by those clever enough to see them - he would need to have assumed two things:
1) That the murder scene was going to be photographed
2) That the picture taken would be from such an angle that the initials on the wall would be clearly in line of sight.
The other pictures we have of victims are post mortem photographs taken in the mortuary, not in situ at the murder scene. How could the killer have known that a photographer would be hired to photograph the body in the room and so record the initials for all time? If the photographer had chosen or been instructed to take the photograph from the foot of the bed, or, as in the case of the other victims, as a close up of the face, the initials would not have been visible and a record of them

would have been lost forever. It seems much more likely to me that a later observer, noticing the semblance of initials in what were actually random markings on the wall or the photograph, extrapolated the story of the initials from the perspective of the killer in a manner which the murderer, at the time of the killing and its aftermath, could not have known would be preserved in this way for future generations to see.

So, these are some of the alleged mysteries attending the killing of Mary Kelly. They have been debated at meticulous length and I am sure this heated discussion will continue. Of course, I do not claim to have "solved" any of these points - if such a solution at this remove in time is possible. But I have tried to look at them logically and to assess what would have been the most feasible background to each occurrence in the light of the statements made at the time. These matters will not be laid to rest nor, perhaps, should they be because healthy debate should be a part of any investigation or consideration of the Whitechapel murders. But that debate should, in my opinion, always be tempered by what is probable or even, on occasion, possible.

Chapter 6

George Hutchinson's Story

The inquest into the murder of Mary Kelly started and finished on the 12th of November, 1888. About 6 p.m. on that evening, just a short time after the inquest jury had returned its predictable verdict of "Murder against some person or persons unknown," a man walked into the Commercial Street police station and made a statement which, if made earlier, would have been most pertinent to the inquest at which he would almost certainly been called as a witness had he come forward before. There has been a huge amount of debate about this man and the evidence he gave. His name was George Hutchinson. Briefly put, his story was that he met Kelly while he was wandering the streets at 2 a.m. on the morning of the murder and she asked him for money. He was unable to oblige her and, as she wandered off, she was approached by another man with whom she went back to Miller's Court. Hutchinson followed them and waited about outside for, in his estimation, about 45 minutes before finally leaving. Hutchinson's description of the man he saw with Kelly was not only much more detailed than any previous sighting of a man seen with a victim shortly before a murder, but is considered by many simply too detailed to be true, considering this was an alleged view of a man at 2 a.m. in the open street.

The official documents consist of Hutchinson's signed statement and an account, also dated the 12th of November, of an interview Abberline had with Hutchinson. Neither gives any detail about Hutchinson except for his address which at the time of the murder was quoted as the Victoria Home, Commercial Street. Not even his age or trade is given. Had he been called as an inquest witness these bare details might have been forthcoming, but this was not to be the case. Press accounts frequently describe Hutchinson as a groom but a search under his name of both the 1881 and 1891 censuses failed to reveal anyone described as a groom, horse keeper or any similar occupation. The Daily News of 13th November has this to say about Hutchinson : "A man, apparently of the labouring class, but of a military appearance, who knew the

81

deceased, last night lodged with the police a long and detailed statement of an incident which attracted his attention on the day in question." The interview with Abberline does add some important details that are not mentioned in his witness statement. He told Abberline that he had occasionally given Kelly a few shillings and had known her about three years. Of course, how Kelly and Hutchinson had become acquainted is not known, but the alleged length of his knowing her is important in that of all the witnesses that testified about Kelly, Hutchinson, if his statement to Abberline is true, would have known her by far the longest. Even Joe Barnett, the man with whom she had lived until shortly before the murder, had only known her eighteen months. There has been speculation that there was some hidden connection, even possibly a family connection, between Kelly and John McCarthy, her landlord. However the provable length of their acquaintance was only that time which she and Barnett had occupied the room at Miller's Court, estimated at the inquest as about eight months.

Apart from the minimal background we learn about Hutchinson himself, we can split the information from the three available sources - the witness statement, the Abberline interview, and press accounts - into three main areas. These are:
1) The account of Hutchinson's meeting with Kelly
2) The description of the man seen with Kelly
3) What Hutchinson did after the meeting of Kelly and the man.
How Hutchinson came to be walking the streets is explained in a press interview of the 14th of November. He had been to Romford (some accounts said to visit his sister) and had walked all the way back to Whitechapel by which time the Victoria Home was closed so he walked the streets all night even after the meeting with Kelly and the man. As he himself is quoted as putting it: "After I left the court I walked about all night, as the place where I usually sleep was closed. I came in as soon as it opened in the morning. I am able to fix the time, as it was between ten and five minutes to two o'clock as I came by Whitechapel Church. When I left the corner of Miller's court the clock struck three o'clock." The logistics and sequence of events do vary between the witness statement and the press account. In his police statement, Hutchinson

says he saw Kelly just before Flower and Dean Street. She asked him for money and he said he was unable to oblige. She walked off towards Thrawl Street and a man coming in the opposite direction approached her. However, in his press interview, Hutchinson claimed to have seen the man first and then Kelly: "As I passed Thrawl street I passed a man standing at the corner of the street, and as I went towards Flower and Dean street I met the woman Kelly, whom I knew very well, having been in her company a number of times ...... The man who was standing at the corner of Thrawl street then came towards her." If Hutchinson was a hoaxer or a publicity seeker then he was certainly taking a considerable risk in that his statement, in effect, says the following:

1) He was, with the exception of the killer, the last person to see and talk to Kelly alive, if we accept the conventional chronology of the night of the murder, and not that of Caroline Maxwell (of whom more later.)

2) He was at or very near to the scene of the murder for at least 45 minutes on his own admission.

3) He was wandering the streets of Whitechapel all night and therefore, almost by definition, he would not be able to provide a substantial alibi for himself.

When Hutchinson met Kelly she asked him to lend her sixpence. Hutchinson told Abberline he had known her about three years and that he had "occasionally given the deceased a few shillings." His relationship with Kelly is described in the Daily News of 14th November as follows: "I met the woman Kelly, whom I knew very well, having been in her company a number of times." This inevitably raises the question of what was the nature of Hutchinson's connection with Kelly. Was he a casual client of hers which would explain why he had been in her company and given her money? Barnett testified that before he knew Kelly she had earned her living by prostitution, so Hutchinson being a client of hers is not wildly improbable, and almost certainly he would not have admitted to it, knowing that whatever he said would appear widely in print. However, we cannot take it as proven. The possibility exists that Kelly and Hutchinson were casual friends and he helped her out when he could. Both possibilities are tenable and neither is currently provable. There is also the seemingly odd statement in Hutchinson's press interview: "My suspicions were aroused by seeing a man so well dressed, but I had no suspicion that he was the murderer." If he did not suspect this man of being the Whitechapel murderer, then what exactly were his suspicions? Why did he observe him in such obsessive detail and follow the couple to Miller's Court and then stand outside the entrance to the court for about forty five minutes? Depending on one's interpretation of the nature of his relationship with Kelly, it could be that he was jealous or that he was worried for her safety. If he was a client of Kelly's, was he frustrated that he did not have the money to enjoy her company that night? Did he stare fixedly at the well dressed man to try and deter him so that Kelly would be free to entertain him if no money were forthcoming? Also we must not forget that Hutchinson was homeless for the night, the Victoria Home having closed its doors by the time he got back to Whitechapel. Even if he were not hoping to enjoy Kelly's sexual favours, was he perhaps hoping she would give him a roof over his head for the rest of the night to save him the dreary trudge round Whitechapel till dawn.

The description of the man allegedly seen with Kelly is by far the most detailed given by any witness during the murders. Is it too detailed, simply too good to be true? It has been argued that it would simply not have been possible to have noted so much detailed information by the light of Victorian streetlamps at 2 o'clock in the morning. There is also the time lag between the observation and its being reported - somewhere about 88 hours, from 2 a.m. on the morning of the 9th November until 6 p.m. on the evening on the 12th of November. Of course, what is not known is how long the couple were together in Hutchinson's sight. According to his statement, they met near the corner of Thrawl Street and, after some conversation there, walked slowly back past Hutchinson and then crossed over to Dorset Street. They stood, by his estimation, outside the entrance to Miller's Court for about three minutes and then went up the court to Kelly's room. So it is possible that Kelly and the man were observed by Hutchinson for somewhere about five or six minutes. This is certainly in contrast to other sightings such as those in Hanbury Street and near Mitre Square, which were literally passing glances. Also what is unique in Hutchinson's testimony is that he knew and spoke to the woman involved, whereas in other sightings the woman was unknown to the witness so they had no personal motive to be any more observant that one would usually be passing someone casually in the street. So perhaps we have been over critical of Hutchinson's powers of observation. He stood for about five or six minutes observing a man who was with a woman he knew and, perhaps, whose company he would have liked to have enjoyed himself. That length of time would allow for reasonably detailed observation and we cannot dismiss his testimony simply because it is so exact. Another thing we most not forget is that human powers of observation and recall vary widely from one person to another. We simply have no way of knowing if Hutchinson was one of those blessed by nature with a strong ability to note and recall detail after the event.

If we look at the description in Hutchinson's police statement and that which he is quoted as giving in the press interview, there are slight discrepancies. In the press interview he says:

"The man was about 5ft 8in in height and 34 or 35 years of age, with dark complexion and dark moustache turned up at the ends. He was wearing a long dark coat trimmed with astrachan, a white collar with black necktie, in which was affixed a horseshoe pin. He wore a pair of dark "spats" with light buttons over button boots, and displayed from his waistcoat a massive gold chain. His watch chain had a big seal with a red stone hanging from it. He had a heavy moustache, curled up, and dark eyes and bushy eyebrows. He had no side whiskers, and his chin was clean shaven. He looked like a foreigner." In the police statement, he assesses the man's height as 5ft 6in and he does not mention the seal with a red stone hanging from the watch chain. The wording of the press statement may clarify one minutely detailed observation that has been questioned in what he told the police. In his deposition to the authorities, he said that the man had "dark eyes and eye lashes," and it has been asked how anyone could have noted the colour of someone's eyelashes out in the street at two o'clock in the morning. In the press report this has become "dark eyes and bushy eyebrows," which is possibly what he said or meant to say to the police as it is an altogether more likely observation. The last discrepancy is that the man's appearance in the press is described as "a foreigner," but in his police statement he specifically says that he had a "Jewish appearance."

Two related questions are what Hutchinson did after he left the environs of Miller's Court and why it took him so long to go the police station to report what he had seen. On the first matter, as we have already seen, he specifically said that he was effectively homeless for the night as the Victoria Home had closed its doors, and he wandered the streets for the rest of the night. Whether he returned to or near Miller's Court at any point in his wanderings is not revealed. As Hutchinson says in the press article: "After I left the court I walked about all night, as the place where I usually sleep was closed. I came in as soon as it opened in the morning." As to what Hutchinson did between his sighting and the visit to Commercial Street police station, he summarises this as follows: "I was out last night until three o'clock looking for him. I could swear to the man anywhere. I told one policeman on Sunday morning what I had seen, but did not go to the police station. I told one of the lodgers here about it yesterday, and he advised me to go to the police station, which I did last night." The "last night" referred to here is the evening of Monday, the 12th November, so Hutchinson is saying he went out after visiting the police and talking to Abberline until the early hours of the morning. This may have been in the company of police officers, as Abberline says in the report of his interview that "arrangement was at once made for two officers to accompany him round the district for a few hours tonight with a view of finding the man if possible." What made Hutchinson think he had a chance of seeing the man by random wanderings in the street? He himself says "I believe that he lives in the neighbourhood, and I fancied that I saw him in Petticoat lane on Sunday morning, but I was not certain." Initially it would seem unlikely that a man of the description given by Hutchinson would live in the Whitechapel area, but we must not fall into thinking that every inch of the area consisted of stinking alleyways and slum lodging houses. There were many successful businesses in the area, and the census returns and trade directories for the period show that there was a sizeable number of professional people living in certain parts of the neighbourhood. We are informed he told a policeman about his sighting on the Sunday, that is the 11th of November. As he says specifically that he did not go to the police station on that day, this would very probably refer to a policeman on the beat, though who and of what rank is not known. Finally it was the urging of one of his fellow inmates at the Victoria Home on the Monday that prompted him to visit the police station and report what he knew. Unless Hutchinson never read a newspaper and listened to no talk in the streets he can hardly have been unaware that a new murder had occurred. The location of this had been widely reported as Miller's Court and the victim's name as Kelly. Whether some rational reason prevented Hutchinson from finding out about the murder - for example, that he may have been away for the weekend - or whether he had some personal reason for his reluctance in coming forward we cannot know. The final act in his participation was his attending the mortuary to view the body. Abberline says in his report that Hutchinson had been asked to do this and he himself confirms it in his press interview - "I went down to the Shoreditch mortuary today and recognised the body as being that of the woman Kelly, whom I saw at two o'clock on Friday morning." The purpose of this was obviously not formal identification of the deceased, as the inquest was already over, but to confirm that the woman he was talking about in his statement and the deceased were one and the same.

So who was Hutchinson? As we have seen, the available reports give no firm indication of his trade or age. Abberline's report says only that he was "at present in no regular employment," and the Daily News interview states that he was "George Hutchinson, a groom by trade, but now working as a labourer." Again we have the mention of his trade as a groom but, as already stated, the 1891 census lists no George Hutchinson with such an occupation. One allegedly firm identification of Hutchinson was made by Melvyn Fairclough in his book "The Ripper and the Royals." It is asserted that he was one George William Topping Hutchinson and the book includes an interview with his son Reginald who claimed that his father told him that he knew one of the women killed by the Ripper and had been interviewed by the police. Certainly George William Topping Hutchinson did exist and we can trace a certain amount of detail about him and his background. His birth was registered in Lambeth in the last quarter of 1866 and so the first view we have of him in the census data is in 1871, when the address and details of the family are given as follows:

5 Champney Terrace, Norwood, Lambeth
Head:
George Hutchinson aged 24 (sic) born Chelmsford, Essex - Plumber
Wife:
Jane Hutchinson aged 39 born Cambridge
Children:
George aged 4 born Surrey
Jane aged 10 born Hornchurch, Essex
Lodgers:
Henry Goswell aged 23 born Middlesex - Carter
William Mayhew aged 38 born Clanfield, Essex - Carter
Thomas Sullivan aged 23 born Ireland
Savina Sullivan aged 22 born Tottenham
William Bailey aged 38 born Sussex - Gasfitter
Ellen Bailey aged 23 born Lewes, Sussex

The reported age of George Snr. is oddly awry, and should read, in 1871, 44 years of age. This is confirmed by subsequent census entries and the unlikely possibility of a 24 year old man having a 10 year old daughter. It will be seen that Hutchinson had only one sibling. The birth of his sister, listed in the census as born in Hornchurch, is probably referred to in the listing in the second quarter of 1861, that of a Jane Emily Hutchinson born in Romford. By 1881, the mother of the two children had died, and George and his sister were still living with their father, albeit at a different address:

4 Roper Street, Eltham, Kent.
Head:
George Hutchinson aged 54 born Chelmsford, Essex
Plumber
Widowed
Children:
Jane Hutchinson aged 19 born Hornchurch, Essex
Housekeeper
George W. Hutchinson aged 14 born Norwood, Surrey
Scholar.

As George Snr is listed as widowed in 1881, his wife, Jane, must have died at some time between the censuses of 1871 and 1881. In 1871 the family was living in Lambeth, so it is possible the death would have been registered there. There are two possible entries in that range of years where the age at death is approximate to what we would have expected from the census. In the 3rd Quarter of 1872 the death was registered at Lambeth (1d 291)of a Jane Hutchinson aged 38. The 1871 census would have indicated her age in that year to be 40. In the third quarter of 1881 the death of a Jane Elizabeth Hutchinson was registered, also at Lambeth (1d 225) aged 46. The age as calculated from the previous census would have been 48. But by the time of this second death, the 1881 census would have already taken place, so the former entry seems more likely.

By 1891 the family had split up. George Snr. had remarried and had fathered another son.
Address:
4 Lenham Road, Lee, London
Head:
George Hutchinson aged 63 born Chelmsford, Essex
Plumber
Wife:
Emma Hutchinson aged 41 born Upton
Son:
Herbert Hutchinson aged 1 born Lee, Kent
Niece:
Agnes M. Wratton aged 14 born Lee, Kent
George William Hutchinson is listed as living at a lodging house at 69 Warren Street, Tottenham Court, London.
His details are given as follows:
George W.T. Hutchinson aged 24 born Norwood, London
(The initials are given in the index as G.W.S. but comparison with the enumerator's writing shows this should be G.W.T.)
Lodger
Single
Plumber

I have as yet not been able to find Jane Hutchinson, George's sister, in the 1891 census or any record of a marriage for her between 1881 and 1891. Between the returns for 1891 and 1901 George William married. This took place in the second quarter of 1898:

The marriage was registered at Mile End between George William T Hutchinson and Florence Jervis (Volume 1c Page 806)

Florence Jervis was the daughter of John Jervis, a sawyer, born in Bursledon, Hampshire in 1841 and Susan Jervis born Swansea, Wales, in 1845. Addresses for the family so far traced are:

1891 - 189 Manchester Street, Poplar

1881 - 57 Rhodeswell Street, London.

George William with his wife and young family are listed in 1901 as follows:

80 Tower Street, St George the Martyr, London

Head:

George Hutchinson aged 35 born Surrey - Plumber

Wife:

Florence Hutchinson aged 32 born Middlesex

Children:

George aged 2

Albert aged 1

Both born in Middlesex.

This individual certainly has many family ties with Essex and it is intriguing that the Hutchinson of the Kelly case had been visiting Romford on the evening before the murder. Some reports claim he had been visiting his sister, but her whereabouts in the 1891 census have yet to be established. It will be interesting to see if she lived in or near Romford at that time. The main stumbling block to the identification of George William Topping Hutchinson as the man interviewed by Abberline is that of his trade. George William's son said his father was a plumber from a family of plumbers, and the census information consistently identifies him as following this trade. The suggestion that he was a groom was only found in press reports and is present nowhere in the police statements. Abberline says only that at the time of the interview he was in "no regular employment." This, of course, could be consistent with any trade and all we can say at present is that nothing in the two police statements conflicts with the idea of Hutchinson being a plumber. Where the idea came from that he was, or had been, a groom is unknown and may well be wrong information picked up by the press.

There has been much speculation about Hutchinson and his role in the investigation of Kelly's murder. The crucial question, of course, is what, if anything, did he see and how much did he embellish his description, if at all, and if so to what purpose? I can see no grounds per se from the available documentation for concluding that Hutchinson was either implicated in any way in Kelly's murder or entirely inventing his testimony. However, there remain certain question marks over his evidence to which we would dearly love to know the answers:

1) Why did he delay so long in coming forward with his information?

2) Was he aware of the murder over the intervening weekend or was he away from the area?

3) Why did he take such a close interest in Kelly and her companion and wait about so long outside Miller's Court?

4) What was the nature of his relationship with Kelly - client or friend?

These points will almost certainly never be answered and the role and reliability of George Hutchinson must remain to an appreciable extent a matter of speculation.

Chapter 7

Kelly Rises from the Dead: Caroline Maxwell and Others

We now come to one of the oddest aspects of an odd case! Put simply, two witnesses claimed to have seen Kelly out and about on the streets near Miller's Court hours after the time when medical and circumstantial evidence suggested she had been killed. The first of these, who gave a police statement and testified at the Kelly inquest, was Caroline Maxwell. The second, who was quoted in press reports but did not give official evidence, was Maurice Lewis. The stories told by these two witnesses have caused much consternation and have given rise to elaborate theorising, most of it centring on the idea that the woman killed in Miller's Court was not, if fact, Kelly, but that she survived and was seen the next morning.

We must look at what these two people actually said they had seen. Mrs. Caroline Maxwell described herself as the wife of Henry Maxwell who was, in her account, the deputy of a lodging house at 14 Dorset Street. I say "in her account" because I have been unable to find a couple named Henry and Caroline Maxwell in either the 1881 or 1891 census, and have to date failed to find any record of their marriage. Of course, it is possible that Henry and Caroline were not actually married, but in that case if they were living together as man and wife in either 1881 or 1891 I would have expected the census to show them as such. Whatever their marital status, Mrs. Maxwell said in her police statement, dated 9th November, that she had seen Kelly standing at the entrance of Miller's Court, her exact words being "I had not seen her for three weeks until Friday morning 9th about half past 8 o'clock." Mrs. Maxwell had a brief conversation with Kelly. When she returned to Dorset Street at about 9 a.m. she again saw Kelly standing outside the Britannia public house talking to a man. We will look at the content of what was said later, but at the moment the critical and puzzling aspect of these events is their chronology.

The second witness who claimed to have seen Kelly on the morning of the 9th of November is quoted in press accounts as being a tailor named Maurice Lewis, but this version of his forename is almost certainly an error. His name was actually Morris Lewis and he is listed in 1891 as living at 21 Spelman Street, Spitalfields. He and his household are given as follows:

Head: Morris Lewis aged 50 born Russia - Tailor
Wife: Rachel Lewis aged 47 born Russia
Daughter: Sarah Lewis aged 11 born Russia
Lodger: Sarah Cohen aged 26 born Poland - Fan sewer

Lewis claimed that he had seen Kelly drinking in the Britannia at about 10 a.m. on the morning of the murder. Lewis also claimed that on the previous evening he had seen Kelly drinking in the Horn of Plenty public house with "Julia," the mysterious fellow prostitute Kelly had offered shelter to, and a man identified as Danny which press sources identified as a nickname for Joseph Barnett. However, it has been suggested more recently that this may in fact have been Barnett's brother, Daniel. The other noteworthy feature of Lewis's press statement is that he had known Kelly for five years. This is longer than Hutchinson had claimed to have known her, and in fact would take Lewis's alleged acquaintance with Kelly back to 1883, which predates the time when Barnett claimed she moved to London. Is Lewis claiming that he knew her while she still lived in Wales? Or is there some more down to earth explanation, for example that Lewis claimed five months' acquaintance, and not five years?

All of these claims make it necessary to look at the alleged chronology of events on the night of Kelly's murder. We will try to fit existing statements into a time framework which is crucial to addressing the central question to try and resolve the claims of Maxwell and Lewis - i.e. at what time did Mary Kelly die? From the claims and statements of the various witnesses who said they saw Kelly on the evening of the 8th or the morning of the 9th of November, we get the following alleged chronology:

8th November:
10 a.m. - Julia Venturney sees Kelly having breakfast in her room with another woman.

Afternoon: Maria Harvey claimed that she and Kelly were together all the afternoon.

6.55 p.m. - Maria Harvey claims this was the last time she saw Kelly in her room and that Barnett arrived at this time.

7.00 p.m. to 8 p.m. - Barnett visited Kelly in her room and said there was a woman there with Kelly when he arrived.

Evening - Maurice Lewis claimed he saw Kelly, Julia and "Danny" (possibly Joseph Barnett) drinking in the Horn of Plenty public house at the corner of Crispin Street and Dorset Street.

11.45 p.m. - Mary Ann Cox entered Dorset Street and saw Kelly walking in front of her with a man. This time is taken from her police statement, but at the inquest she gave the time as 12.00 midnight.

9th November:

12.00 - 12.15 - Mary Ann Cox leaves Miller's Court and hears Kelly singing in her room.

1.00 - Mary Ann Cox again goes out and Kelly is still singing.

1.00 - 1.30 - Elizabeth Prater stands at the entrance to Miller's Court, talking for a short time to John McCarthy. At the inquest Prater gave the times she was at this spot as 1.00 to 1.20.

2.00 - George Hutchinson meets Kelly near Flower and Dean Street.

2.00 - 3.00 - Sarah Lewis arrives at Miller's Court and sees a man standing outside the lodging house opposite the entrance to Miller's Court. In her inquest testimony Sarah Lewis gave her time of arrival as 2.30.

2.05 (approximately) - Hutchinson sees Kelly and the man she met standing at the entrance to Miller's Court.

2.08 (approximately) - Hutchinson sees Kelly and the man enter Miller's Court and go into her room.

2.50 to 3.00 - Hutchinson leaves the entrance to Miller's Court.

3.00 - Mary Ann Cox returns to Miller's Court. There is no light in Kelly's room and all is quiet.

3.30 - 4.00 - Elizabeth Prater in the room above Kelly's is awakened and hears two or three screams in a female voice of "Murder."

3.45 - 4.00 - Sarah Lewis hears a cry of "Murder" in a female voice.

5.45 - Mary Ann Cox hears someone leave Miller's Court.

8.30 - Caroline Maxwell sees Kelly standing at the entrance to Miller's

Court and speaks with her briefly. It should be noted that in the police statement the time was entered as a marginal note and at the inquest Maxwell gave the time as 8.00 to 8.30.

9.00 - Maxwell sees Kelly standing outside the Britannia public house at the corner of Dorset Street talking to a man. In her inquest testimony she estimates this sighting at 8.45.

10.00 - Maurice Lewis sees Kelly in the Britannia public house.

10.45 - Bowyer finds Kelly's body in her room at Miller's Court.

During this time Kelly was allegedly seen in the company of a man by the following witnesses:

Mary Ann Cox - saw Kelly enter her room with a man about midnight. About 36 years of age, 5ft 5in in height.

Caroline Maxwell - saw Kelly with a man about 9 a.m. on the 9th. Age about 30 years of age, 5ft 5in in height.

Hutchinson - saw Kelly meet a man in Commercial Street. Age 34 or 35, height 5ft 6in.

We now come to the vexed question of the time of Kelly's death. It must be noted that at the inquest the only medical man who gave evidence was Dr. Phillips and his deposition in the inquest papers does not include an estimate of the time of death. The post mortem report as signed by Dr. Thomas Bond, whilst including a very detailed list of the injuries, does not include an estimate of the time when death occurred. When looking at the time of death we have certain factors to bear in mind:

1) Although the body was found at 10.45 a.m., the room was not entered, on Phillips' testimony, until 1.30 p.m.

2) At the time of Kelly's murder, estimation of time of death was more an art than a science. It was based on a combination of rigor mortis (if present) and algor mortis, the reduction of body temperature after death until it matches the surrounding air temperature. In current practice the time of death from body temperature is estimated using a formula called the Glaister equation. This is expressed as follows: 98.4 degrees Fahrenheit minus the rectal temperature of the body divided by 1.5 gives the number of hours elapsed since death. However even today this is used only as a guide and the result can be skewed by other factors.

3) Kelly's murder took place in early November, a cold time of year, which means the ambient temperature may well have been relatively low, especially in a room with a broken window. There had been a fire in the room but we have no way to know the time or duration of this blaze.

4) The gross mutilations of Kelly's body had eviscerated and partially skinned the corpse. This would have opened to the ambient air temperature many surfaces which in a less visceral killing would have cooled more slowly as they would have remained enclosed within the body cavity.

So, the estimated time of death from contemporary sources cannot give us any guide as to when Kelly died. A most relevant article on this subject, which appeared in Ripperoo magazine, written by Cherise McClain, Carl Dodd & Julian Rosenthal and entitled "ESTIMATING MARY KELLY'S TIME OF DEATH" has some very interesting observations. Although Dr. Bond does not mention time of death in his post mortem report on Kelly, another report dated the 10th of November which compares four of the killings, he has this to say, which gives much more detail:

"In the Dorset Street case the body was lying on the bed at the time of my visit, 2 o'clock, quite naked and mutilated as in the annexed report. Rigor mortis had set in but increased during the course of the examination. From this it is difficult to say with any degree of certainty the exact time that had elapsed since death as the period varies from six to twelve hours before rigidity sets in. The body was comparatively cold at 2 o'clock and the remains of a recently taken meal were found in the stomach and scattered about over the intestines. It is therefore pretty certain that the woman must have been dead about 12 hours and the partly digested food would indicate that death took place about 3 or 4 hours after the food was taken, so one or two o'clock in the morning would be the probable time of the murder." The authors of the Ripperoo article qualify Bond's estimate by saying that, in their estimation, rigor mortis peaked at 3 p.m. which leads them to suggest a time of death of 3.00 to 3.30 a.m. Their general comments on rigor mortis note that it sets in as a general rule after 3 to 4 hours and "peaks" after about 12 hours. However, they do note that certain factors can slow or accelerate its onset. Among these they include air temperature and moisture in the air.

Even today there is much disagreement about the onset and duration of rigor mortis. Of the sources I have consulted the following estimates were but a few of the variations:
1) Onset 3 hours after death - duration 26 hours. (deathonline.net)
2) Onset 10 minutes to several hours - duration 72 hours (chemistry. about.com)
3) Onset 10 minutes to several hours - duration 24 hours (Columbia Encyclopaedia)
4) Onset several hours - duration 48 hours (Explainthat.info)
These are only a few among many opinions on the subject.
So Dr. Bond in the passage referring to time of death cites three factors - body temperature, rigor mortis and the remains of a meal in the digestive tract. On the first of these, Bond says the body was "comparatively cold" at 2 o'clock but appears to make no further use of body temperature as a guide to time of death. With regard to rigor mortis, Bond specifically says "Rigor mortis had set in but increased during the course of the examination. From this it is difficult to say with any degree of certainty the exact time that had elapsed since death as the period varies from six to twelve hours before rigidity sets in," but then proceeds to say "It is therefore pretty certain that the woman must have been dead about 12 hours." These two statements blatantly contradict each other, and the only other factor mentioned between them is the placing of the remains of Kelly's last meal within her digestive system. In my opinion, the only resolution of this is that Bond was basing the certainty of his 12 hour estimate on the likely time Kelly took her last meal, a fact which he could not possibly have known.

There is one statement in the Ripperoo article with which I must disagree. The authors say that Bond started his autopsy at 2 p.m. All sources which mention the autopsy agree that it took place at Shoreditch Mortuary and involved the reconstruction, as far as this was possible, of the remains to ascertain if anything was missing. The medics present at Miller's Court entered the room at about 1.30 pm and the remains were removed some four hours later. However, I would suggest that some of Bond's observations, such as those relating to stomach contents and placing of food remains in the intestines, would not have been carried out in situ at Miller's Court but would have been reserved for the full examination at Shoreditch.

One final piece of circumstantial as opposed to medical evidence which has been used in an attempt to place the time of Kelly's death is the fact that two of the witnesses reported hearing a cry of "Murder" in a female voice at approximately the same time. Elizabeth Prater said she heard two or three such cries at 3.30 or 4.00 a.m. She had just been woken and how she estimated this time is not known from her police statement. However, in her inquest testimony this statement is qualified in two respects, as she deposed "I noticed the lodging house light was out, so it was after four probably. It is nothing uncommon to hear cries of murder so I took no notice - I did not hear it a second time." So both the time and number of the cries are uncertain. The lodging house she refers to as her reference point for estimating the time is also mentioned in her police statement, albeit with no reference to the lights being out - "I did not take much notice of such cries as I frequently hear such cries from the back of the lodging house where the windows look into Miller's Court." Logically this can only refer to the lodging house at 28 and 29 Dorset Street, next door to McCarthy's shop. In both 1881 and 1891 this establishment is listed as under the proprietorship of Alexander McQueen and his wife Ann. The other witness who reported a cry was Sarah Lewis, who heard a single cry shortly before 4 o'clock. The variations between these timings is small and it seems reasonably certain that both women, some time shortly before or after 4 a.m., heard a single cry in a female voice. Of course, whether or not this was Kelly is a very different question indeed. However, we must remember that witnesses repeatedly state in evidence throughout the period of the murders that such cries were so common that no notice was taken of them. As Elizabeth Prater was sleeping in the room above Kelly she should have been well placed to state with certainty whether the cry or cries came from the room below. But all she said in her inquest testimony was that the cry seemed to come from "close by."

Where does this leave Caroline Maxwell's testimony? The concensus of opinion is summed up in Philip Sugden's excellent book "The Complete History of Jack the Ripper" when he mentions the possibilities that she was lying, drunk or mistaken. We must look at each possibility in turn:

1) Maxwell was lying. If this were the case the obvious question would be what was her motive? The usual motives for such action in a high profile murder case would be notoriety or financial gain. There is no evidence that Maxwell gained either. She was not, as far as can be traced, interviewed by the press so the extent of any notoriety would be limited to the inquest hearing itself. In the full inquest transcript as reported in the Daily Telegraph of November 13th, the Coroner specifically warned her to be careful about her evidence as it was at variance with other testimony. He said "You must be very careful about your evidence, because it is different to other people's. You say you saw her standing at the corner of the entry to the court ?" to which Maxwell replied "Yes, on Friday morning, from eight to half-past eight. I fix the time by my husband's finishing work. When I came out of the lodging-house she was opposite." Later in her cross examination by the Coroner, Maxwell said, regarding her alleged second sighting of Kelly that morning, "I am sure it was the deceased. I am willing to swear it." The Coroner rightly reminded her "You are sworn now." This was Dr. McDonald's reminder to her that lying under oath at a Coroner's Court, just as in a criminal court, constitutes perjury and was and is a very serious offence. Would she have been willing to risk this for what seems to be very little if any personal return? Also we must remember that unlike some other spectacular evidence like that of George Hutchinson, which came to light days after the murder, Maxwell's evidence was on file with the police from the very beginning of the investigation.

2) Maxwell was drunk. The itinerary of Maxwell which caused her to be in and around Dorset Street at the times she claimed was because her working day had started and she was about her normal business. Her husband was deputy at a lodging house opposite the entrance to Miller's Court. Incidentally, this was presumably the same establishment outside which Sarah Lewis saw a man standing on the morning of the murder. It was Maxwell's custom to go to the house between 8 and 8.30 in

the morning, as she says this was how she judged the time when she collected the plates from her husband's place of work. It was while she was doing this that she saw Kelly at the entrance to Miller's Court. After her brief conversation with Kelly she left to go on an errand to Bishopsgate to get her husband's breakfast and on her return to Dorset Street, which she estimated at about 8.45 she saw Kelly again outside the Britannia talking to a man. This mundane routine does not sound like the actions of a woman so drunk that she would be incapable of even knowing what day it was. The statements and the actions of Maxwell as reported simply do not allow the interpretation, in my opinion, that she was incapable with drink.

3) Maxwell was mistaken. The usual interpretation of this option is not that she was mistaken about seeing Kelly and speaking to her, but that she had the wrong day. This version suggests that the events described by Maxwell may well have happened but it must have been on the Thursday morning, or even earlier in the week, and not on the Friday when the body was found. This seems logical enough but there is one huge stumbling block to this interpretation of Maxwell's testimony. As stated already, Maxwell did not, like Hutchinson, come forward some days later but was interviewed by the police and made a statement at the very beginning of the investigation. Her statement, like those still extant, is dated the 9th of November. In other words, she was interviewed on the very day of the murder. The events she was describing had happened that very morning. It stretches credibility to the extreme to suggest that she became so confused that she mistook events from the previous day or even earlier with what had happened on the very morning of the day she was being questioned about. It may seem odd that Maxwell refers to the day in question as "Friday morning 9th" instead of "today" or "this morning." Mary Ann Cox refers to "last night," Sarah Lewis to "this morning" and Maria Harvey "last night." However, other witnesses refer to the day of the murder, the day they were being interviewed, more formally. Thomas Bowyer refers to the "9th instant" and Elizabeth Prater says that she "returned about 1 a.m. 9th." So this way of referring to the very day when they were being interviewed cannot be taken as evidence in Maxwell's case that she had got the wrong day.

The story told by Maurice Lewis is frustrating in that his account only appeared in the press. There is no police statement available nor was he called at the inquest and his testimony subjected to scrutiny by the Coroner and the jury. We simply do not know whether Lewis would have maintained his story under oath and risked the charge of perjury if it was concocted. The story that he saw Kelly and two companions drinking on the previous evening does not of itself raise problems. It is the assertion that he saw Kelly drinking in the Britannia at 10 a.m. on the morning of the murder which raises severe doubts. Although the alleged second sighting by Maxwell placed Kelly outside the Britannia and Lewis allegedly saw her inside drinking, there is a one and a quarter hour time difference between the two sightings. If Maxwell did see Kelly, there is a two hour difference between her seeing Kelly the second time and the body being found. But in the case of Lewis' story this gap narrows to only forty five minutes.

So where does all this leave us? Difficult though Maxwell's statement is to fit in with the conventional time scheme of events on the 9th of November, none of the usual objections to her version of events is watertight. We cannot say with certainty that she was lying, drunk or mistaken. If she had the right day - the very day she gave her statement - then it must have been Kelly she saw, as she spoke to her and Kelly addressed her by name. Lewis' story must be treated with more caution as it was never given or tested in court, so we have no way of knowing to what extent he would have stuck by it under oath. Also at least one part of his story - that he had known Kelly for five years - is highly suspect in that this predates the commonly agreed date when Kelly moved to London. We would dearly love to know more about the relationship, if any, between Lewis and Kelly and exactly when and how he came forward with his information. There is one last and cryptic mention in the Times of yet another, but unfortunately unnamed witness, who claimed to have seen Kelly during the same time period as Maxwell: "Another young woman, whose name is known, has also informed the police that she is positive she saw Kelly between half-past 8 and a quarter to 9 on Friday morning." As this young woman is not named and this information is included in neither the police statements nor the inquest testimony, it is not possible to pursue this alleged information any further.

The whole question of the time of death and Maxwell's statement is summed up in this same article from The Times of the 12th of November:

"Great difference of opinion exists as to the exact time, or about the time, the murder of Mary Jane Kelly took place. Mrs. Maxwell, the deputy of the Commercial lodging-house, which is situated exactly opposite Miller's-court, the place in which the room of the murdered woman is situated, gave positive information that she saw Mary Jane Kelly standing at the entrance to Miller's-court at half-past 8 on Friday morning. She stated that she expressed surprise at seeing Kelly at that early hour, and asked why she was not in bed. Kelly replied, "I can't sleep. I have the horrors from drink". Mrs. Maxwell further stated that after that she went into Bishopsgate-street to make some purchases, and on her return saw Kelly talking to a short, dark man at the top of the court. When asked by the police how she could fix the time of the morning, Mrs. Maxwell replied, "Because I went to the milk shop for some milk, and I had not before been there for a long time, and that she was wearing a woollen cross-over that I had not seen her wear for a considerable time". On inquiries being made at the milk shop indicated by the woman her statement was found to be correct, and the cross-over was also found in Kelly's room. Against these statements is the opinion of Dr. George Bagster Phillips, the divisional surgeon of the H Division, that when he was called to the deceased (at a quarter to 11) she had been dead some five or six hours. There is no doubt that the body of a person who, to use Dr. Phillip's own words, was "cut all to pieces" would get cold far more quickly than that of one who had died simply from the cutting of the throat; and the room would have been very cold, as there were two broken panes of glass in the windows. Again, the body being entirely uncovered would very quickly get cold. It is the opinion of Mr. M'Carthy [McCarthy], the landlord of 26, Dorset-street, that the woman was murdered at a much earlier hour than 8 o'clock, and that Mrs. Maxwell and the other person must have been mistaken."

It is interesting and perhaps significant that the shop Maxwell claimed she had been to confirmed her visit, suggesting that she had the right day after all. The statement by the Times that Phillips estimated the time of death as five to six hours before 11.15 is obviously in error. Phillips and the other medical men did not gain access to the body, on his own testimony, until 1.30.p.m. The time quoted of 11.15 is the time he arrived at Miller's Court, not the time he started his examination. The article does not make clear whether the estimate of five to six hours allowed for the variable they highlight of ambient temperature and exposed viscera, or whether Phillips was basing this purely on body temperature and the extent of rigor mortis. If Phillips estimated time of death as five to six hours before his examination started, this would place it about 7.30 or 8.30 a.m. If he had not made sufficient allowance for the abnormal features of this murder - the low ambient temperature and extent of mutilation - it means the time of death would have been later than this.

I am not saying that Caroline Maxwell's testimony can be taken at face value. I am simply saying that it cannot be dismissed lightly merely because it is inconvenient. If her story is true it throws, of course, a very different light on the murder at Miller's Court. It would mean that Kelly was killed some time after 8.45 a.m. Since the medical men did not gain entry to her room until 1.30 p.m. this would mean the body would have been lying in situ for up to four and a half hours which certainly falls within the various times quoted for the onset of rigor mortis. If this were true our sights should be set not on Hutchinson's well dressed man, not on the blotchy faced man with the quart of ale but rather on the last man seen with Kelly - standing with her outside the Britannia at 8.45. He was described by Maxwell as follows in her police statement: "About 30, height about 5ft 5in, stout, dressed as a market porter." It may be significant that in her inquest testimony Maxwell's description of this man is markedly different: "The man was not a tall man; he had on dark clothes and a plaid coat. I could not say what hat he had on." Her assertion that he was dressed as a market porter simply does not square with this latter description. She does not specify which type of market porter - most probably either Spitalfields or Billingsgate - but such a man would hardly be likely to wear a plaid coat as his normal working gear. We will consider later the possible significance of why this description changed so markedly.

Chapter 8

Barnett and Other Lovers

Various men are mentioned in the conventional account of Kelly's life as having had a relationship with her. These are, in probable chronological order,

1) The man Davis or Davies to whom she was supposedly legally married

2) The man Morganstone, with whom she lived near Stepney Gas Works, possibly in Pennington Street

3) Joseph Flemming, a mason's plasterer - his address is given as Bethnal Green Road.

4) Joseph Barnett, whom Kelly had met around Easter 1887.

The exact order in which Kelly lived with Morganstone and Flemming is not immediately clear. Barnett, from whom this information came at the inquest, said of these two men : "She told me all this but I do not know which she lived with last." We will take a look at all these men, especially the last, Joseph Barnett, with whom Kelly had been living until a short time before her death and who has in more recent years been put forward as a vigorously supported suspect, at least as the killer of Kelly, if not for the Whitechapel murder series as a whole.

We have already mentioned in an earlier chapter the man Davis or Davies. We have so little information about this alleged husband of Kelly that it is at present not possible to trace him reliably in the available records. This problem is exacerbated by the combination of the surname and location involved, for one could easily rephrase the well known dictum about "looking for a needle in a haystack" to read "looking for a Davies in Wales!" There are a number of surnames - Jones, Davies, Morgan - which are as common in Wales as Smith or Brown are in England. All we can say with certainty at present is that there is no record of a legal marriage within a reasonable period of the reputed date of the event - 1879 - between a Mary Jane Kelly and a man named Davis or Davies. This only leaves a limited number of logical possibilities:

1) The woman's real name under which she married was not Mary Jane Kelly

2) Kelly did legally marry but her husband's name was not Davis or Davies

3) Kelly did know and live with a man named Davies of Davis but the alleged marriage never took place

4) The whole incident was invented by Kelly

5) The whole incident was invented by Barnett

We simply do not have sufficient information at present to determine which of these circumstances reflects what actually happened.

The man Morganstone raises the opposite problem to Davies in that his surname does not appear to exist at all! There is no traceable British record, under census information or Births, Marriages and Deaths, of an individual named Morganstone. It has been theorised that Barnett may have misinterpreted the name as a surname when it should have been a forename and surname i.e. the name should have been rendered as Morgan Stone. But this combination is not helpful either, in that the few occurrences of this name relate to individuals whose ages would make it impossible for them to be the person involved in the Kelly story. Another possibility put forward is that Barnett misheard the name as told to him by Kelly or rendered it in an Anglicised form. The most common forms of known names put forward as possible correct versions of the man's name are Morganstern and Morganstein. But in fact if we look closely at Barnett's words there is an anomaly that may suggest that Kelly lived at two different locations with Morganstone. In the inquest testimony his exact words are quoted as : "She came back and lived in Ratcliffe Highway for some time, she did not tell me how long. Then she was living near Stepney Gas Works. Morganstone was the man she lived with there. She did not tell me how long she lived there. She told me that in Pennington Street she lived at one time with a Morganstone, and with Joseph Flemming, she was very fond of him. He was a mason's plasterer. He lived in Bethnal Green Road." This is most confused. First we are told that Kelly lived near Stepney Gas Works with Morganstone, then that she lived in Pennington Road with both Morganstone and Flemming. How are we to read this? The statement of Barnett's could be interpreted to mean that at one time she was living with both Morganstone and Flemming at Pennington Street, but it is more likely that this menage a trois is more a product of confused wording rather than being his intended meaning. Another possibility is that Kelly lived with Morganstone near Stepney Gas Works and then moved with him to Pennington Street where she later met and moved in with Flemming in the same road. Certainly the two locations are clearly separated and in different areas. Stepney Gas Works was located at the corner of Ben Jonson Road and Harford Street, between Commercial Road and Mile End Road. Pennington Street lay to the southwest and ran parallel to the south of the Ratcliff Highway, later George Street. Certainly this area to the south and west of the Ratcliff Highway is one associated with Kelly's earlier life in more than one account. Two earlier landladies of Kelly were based in this area. Mrs Carthy was said to have been Kelly's landlady in a house in Breezer's Hill which connected Pennington Street and George Street, and Kelly lodged allegedly at some stage with the oddly named Mrs Buki near the western end of George Street. If we list the partners and locations attributed to Kelly we get this puzzling progression:

1) Kelly lived near Stepney Gas Works with Morganstone
2) Kelly lived in Pennington Street (which is not near Stepney Gas Works) with Morganstone and Flemming
3) Flemming lived in Bethnal Green Road.

The logical, but by no means certain, interpretation of this sequence of events is that Kelly first lived near the Gas Works with Morganstone, then move with him to Pennington Street where she met Flemming with whom she subsequently moved to Bethnal Green Road. However, as we shall see, this is not what actually happened.

However, this brings us no nearer to determining who Morganstone was. Neal Stubbings, author of the series of excellent books about the lives and backgrounds of the first four canonical victims, identified the most likely candidate as one Adrianus Morgenstern. There is one definite census listing for this man and his family in 1881. At that stage the address at which he was living was 43 Victoria Road, Fulham, and the family is listed as follows:

Head:

Adrianus L Morgestern (sic) aged 33 born Alphen Priel, Holland - Gas stoker

Wife:

Jeanette aged 28 born Mzerbo(?), Holland

Children:

Johanna C aged 7 born Proogendaal

Maria aged 6 born Proogendaal

Wilhelmina L aged 4 born Fulham

Petronella C aged 3 months born Fulham

Brother (i.e. of head of household):

Maria A Morgestern aged 26 born Alphen Priel, Holland - Gas stoker

The researcher Louis van Dompselaar found fuller details for the family, but the name of the spouse in his research varies from that given in the 1881 census:

Head:

Adrianus Lucas Morgenstern born 1848 in Alphen en Riel

Wife:

Antonetta Smits born 1853 in Meerlo

Children:

Johanna Cornelius born 1873 in Roosendaal

Maria Petronella born 1875 in Roosendaal

Wilhelmina born 1877

Petronella C born 1881 in Fulham

The brother listed as living with the family in 1881 is detailed by Louis van Dompselaar as follows:

Maran (?) Morgenstern born 1855 in Alphen en Riel. In December 1881 he married Florence Charlotte Gilbert at Fulham. The listing of this marriage in the BMD registers gives the groom's name as Marian Morgenstern. The other records relating to this family show that Petronella Carlin Morgenstern died in Fulham in March 1882 at the age of 1.

I have been unable to trace this Morgenstern family in the 1891 record but, oddly, there is one entry that may be connected. At 20

Cordelia Street, Bromley, there is a listed a 43 year old gas stoker named Adrianus Felix, born Rotterdam, Holland. This corresponds with Adrianus Morgenstern with respect to age, trade, forename and country of birth. But his wife is a 27 year old named Elizabeth Felix and they are listed as having a 17 year old daughter named Anna, also listed as born at Rotterdam. This daughter - Anna aged 17 in 1891 - could conceivably be one of his offspring listed in 1881 - Johanna aged 7. Whether Morgenstern changed his name to Felix and remarried cannot be proven at this time.

When we come to Joseph Flemming we are on firmer ground. Brief biographical details were given concerning him in an earlier chapter, but it is now time to look more fully at what can be discovered about him. Firstly the spelling of his name. In census records his name is usually rendered as FLEMMING but in his birth record it is spelt FLEMING. His birth was registered at Bethnal Green in the 2nd Quarter (April to June) of 1859 (Volume 1c page 254). His parents were Richard Fleming, a plasterer, who was born in Ramsgate, Kent in 1822 and Henrietta Fleming, who was born in Camberwell, Surrey in 1822. His mother's maiden name was Henrietta Masom and the couple were married in Lambeth in the 3rd Quarter of 1842 (Volume 4 page 205). Joseph had an elder sister named Jane who was born in Hoxton in 1857, and two younger sisters, Mary Ann born in Bethnal Green in 1863 and Jessie born in Bethnal Green in 1868. The family is listed in the 1871 census living at 60 Wellington Street, Bethnal Green.

By the time of the 1881 census, Joseph had left home and was living in lodgings in 61 Crozier Terrace which was in Homerton, north east of Bethnal Green. By this time he is listed as following his father's trade as a plasterer. His landlady was Ellen Copping, a 35 year old laundress. Also living in the household were Ellen's two daughters - Emily aged 13, and Ann aged 2 - and a second lodger, John Percy, a 27 year old ropemaker, also born in Bethnal Green.

Joseph's family is listed in the 1881 census as living at 4 Cyprus Street and is itemised as follows:

Head:

Richard Fleming aged 59 born Ramsgate, Kent - Plasterer

Wife:

Henrietta Fleming aged 59 born Camberwell, Surrey

Children:

Mary Ann aged 19 born Bethnal Green - Brace machinist (Fancy goods textiles)

Jessie aged 13 born Bethnal Green

Other:

Alice W Rickiam aged 65 born Southsea, Hampshire - Nurse

Emma E Emsworth aged 41 born Lambeth - Lodger

By the time of the 1891 census, Joseph's father, Richard Fleming, is listed as an inmate in the Shoreditch District Infirmary. His details are given as:

Richard Fleming, Married, aged 70, Plasterer, born Ramsgate, Kent.

Richard Fleming's death was registered in Shoreditch in the 1st Quarter of 1894. (Volume 1c Page 59)

In the 1891 Census, Joseph's mother and younger sister are listed as living at 123, Lever Street, City Road as follows:

Head:

Henrietta Fleming aged 69 born Camberwell - Married

Daughter;

Jessie Fleming aged 23 born Bethnal Green - Brace machinist

As for Joseph himself, it looks very much as though he had changed his trade by 1891. At that time he would have been 32 and this, coupled with the fact that he was born in Bethnal Green, led to the only viable identification for him in the 1891 data so far found. This listed him as living in a lodging house at 9 Victoria Park Square, Bethnal Green and gave his details as follows:

Joseph Flemming aged 32 born Bethnal Green - Boot finisher.

This entry lists him as married but no wife is included in the listing for the lodging house. The trade of Boot Finisher is not written in as such but consists of ditto marks from the entry above and I have on occasion found this type of entry to be in error.

By 1901 Joseph's aged mother was still alive and living at 220 Chalk Close, Shoreditch. The household is listed as follows:
Head:
Henrietta Fleming aged 79 born Camberwell
Daughter:
Jessie Fleming aged 33 born Bethnal Green - Brace machinist
Grand daughter:
Henrietta Finch aged 25 born Bethnal Green - Cork factory
At the present time the whereabouts of Joseph Fleming himself in 1901 have not been determined.

We now come to the man central to much recent theorising in the case of the Kelly murder - Joseph Barnett. There are a certainly no lack of entries under this name - for example, the 1891 census lists 36 individuals thus named in London alone. The problem is deciding which of these men is the Joseph Barnett referred to in the Kelly case. We actually learn surprisingly little about him from his police and inquest evidence, not even his age. From these sources we can deduce the following points about Barnett and his background:
1) He had worked as a fish porter, labourer and fruit porter.
2) He had at least one sister.
3) At the time of the murder his sister was living at 21 Portpool Lane, Gray's Inn Road.
4) He had known Kelly and lived with her at various locations for 18-20 months
5) The couple had lived at Miller's Court for about 8 months.
Two leading contenders for identification as the Barnett we are seeking have emerged. The first was postulated by Paul Harrison and was born in 1860 and died in 1927. The second, put forward by Bruce Paley, was born in 1858 and died in 1926.

Paul Harrison tells us the following facts about his contender that should help us to identify him:
1) He was born 23 December 1860

2) He was the second son of David and Maria Barnett. The father was a general dealer.

3) The family resided at 127 Middlesex Street.

4) His parents were devout Catholics.

From this information we are able to trace the family in the 1871 census. It should be noted that at that time they were living at 126 Middlesex Street, not 127.

Head:

David Barnett aged 48 born Whitechapel - General dealer

Wife:

Maria Barnett aged 42 born Holland

Children:

Hannah aged 22

Phoebe aged 18

Abraham aged 16 - Cigar maker

Joseph aged 11

Nancy aged 11

Sarah aged 7

Rachel aged 4

Israel aged 3

Rebecca aged 1

All children were born in Whitechapel.

By the time of the 1881 census David Barnett, the head of the household was dead. The family at this time were listed at 127 Middlesex Street:

Head:

Maria Barnett (Widow) aged 48 born Netherlands - Greengrocer

Children:

Abraham aged 20 - Rivetter

Joseph aged 18 - Rivetter

Nancy aged 17 - Tailoress

Sarah aged 18 - tailoress

Rachel aged 14

Israel aged 11 - Errand boy

Rebecca aged 10

All children born in Whitechapel.

The death of David Barnett is listed in June 1876 in Whitechapel.

Harrison has an odd thing to say about Barnett's meeting with Kelly in 1887: "Barnett fell for the girl instantly who vividly reminded him of his late mother." In fact his mother was still alive and listed in the 1891 census and Joseph was living with her! The family is listed under the surname Barrett, but the details of the family members make the identification with the Barnett family of 1871 and 1881 certain. The remnants of the family were living at 7 Calverley Street, Mile End.

Head:
Maria Barnett (Widow) aged 60 born Rotterdam - General dealer (Shop)
Children:
Joseph aged 28 born Whitechapel - Bootmaker
Israel aged 22 born Whitechapel - Tailor
Rebecca aged 20 born Whitechapel - Tailoress
Servant:
Leah Jacob aged 17 born Spitalfields
Son in Law:
Joseph Benjaman (sic) aged 23 born Whitechapel - Boot maker
In fact, Joseph Benjamin was not yet technically Maria's son in law as he and Rebecca Barnett did not marry until the second quarter of 1891 and Rebecca is still listed in the census of that year as single.

In 1901 Maria Barnett was still living at 7 Calverley Street with one single daughter and one married daughter.
Head:
Maria Barnett (Widow) aged 75 born Rotterdam - general dealer (Shop)
Daughters:
Sarah aged 32 born London
Nancy Burchell aged 36 (Married) born London
Son In Law:
Joseph Burchell aged 37 born London - Clothing traveller
Grandchildren:
Sarah aged 17 - Cigarette maker
David aged 16 - Clothes dealer
Marie aged 13

May aged 11
Hannah aged 9
Leopold aged 2
All born in London.

Joseph's brother Israel had married by 1901 and was living at 17 Beaumont Square, Mile End:

Head:
Israel Barnett aged 31 born Aldgate - Tailor's cutter
Wife:
Hannah Barnett aged 31 born Aldgate
Children:
Marie aged 5
Hannah aged 3
Nancy aged 3 months
All born in Mile End.

Joseph himself I have been unable to trace definitely in 1901 but in this case I think that is not overly important in that we have seen enough of his life and whereabouts to form a judgement on whether this is the Joseph Barnett who lived with Mary Kelly.

Unfortunately I do not think we can say that the man outlined above was the man we are looking for. By way of background, it should be pointed out that the bearers of the surname Barnett in this period in the East End appear to have fallen into two main ethnic groups - Irish and Jewish. Harrison claims that the Barnett he identified was of Irish background and states that Maria Barnett actually moved to Ireland some time after the death of her husband, leaving Joseph to fend for himself. Neither statement can be squared with the facts as revealed in the documents. Not only did Maria Barnett stay in London until at least 1901 but Joseph was living with her until at least 1891. However, the main objection, in my opinion, is the background of the family. The names of their offspring - especially Abraham, Sarah, Israel and Rebecca - display in my opinion an undoubtedly Jewish background. Maria and David Barnett married, according to Harrison, in 1848 and her maiden name was Maria Lazarus. Actually the name is listed in the index as Mary Lazarus. Also we are told she was born in Rotterdam.

All the facts point to Maria being of Dutch Jewish origin and the names of the offspring confirm this identification. Harrison tells us that by the time Barnett met Kelly in early 1887 his mother, Maria, was already dead. I think this is based on a misidentification. A Maria Barnett aged 63 was registered as dead in Whitechapel in March 1887 but the real mother of the Joseph Barnett under examination was certainly still alive in 1891 (he was still living with her) and is still listed in 1901. The last point which causes me problems with this identification of Joseph is the matter of his trade. Harrison tells us that he worked as a fish porter and a fruit porter. In the two available census returns for which Joseph was of a suitable age to have a trade listed (1881 and 1891) he is listed, respectively, as a rivetter and a bootmaker. A rivetter in this context would indicate a boot rivetter, so there is no indication from the evidence we have of Joseph working outside the boot making trade.

We next come to the candidate put forward by Bruce Paley, and I will say from the outset that I think we are here on firmer ground. This Joseph was the son of John and Catherine Barnett, both parents being Irish born. The earliest view we have of the family is in the 1861 census, when they were living at 2 Cartwright Street, Aldgate:

Head:
John Barnett aged 43 born Ireland - Porter at Billingsgate
Wife:
Catherine Barnett aged 40 born Ireland
Children:
Dennis aged 12
Daniel aged 9
Catherine aged 8
Joseph aged 3
John aged 10 months
All children listed as born in Aldgate, City of London
By 1871 both parents were absent, and the second son, Daniel, was listed as head of household, living at 24 and a half, Great Pearl Street, Spitalfields:
Head:
Daniel Barnett aged 20 born Whitechapel - Fishmonger

Sister:

Catherine Barnett aged 17 born Whitechapel

Brothers:

Joseph Barnett aged 13 born Whitechapel

John Barnett aged 9 born Whitechapel

The death of Joseph's father, John, was registered in Whitechapel in the third quarter of 1864 (Vol 1c page 339) but the later whereabouts of his mother, Catherine, remains a mystery. The oldest son, Dennis (also spelt Denis) married in 1869 and his listing in 1871 is as follows:

108 Gosset Street, Bethnal Green

Head:

Denis Barnett aged 22 born Gravesend, Kent - Labourer

Wife:

Mary Ann Barnett aged 21 born Bethnal Green

Daughter:

Mary Ann aged 9 months born Bethnal Green

The one anomaly here is that Denis is listed as born in Gravesend, whereas in 1861 all children of the family were listed as born in Aldgate. This Kent connection may be of significance later.

By 1881 the family had fragmented significantly. The oldest son, Dennis, had moved to Bermondsey and is listed as follows:

5 Goulston's Buildings, Bermondsey

Head:

Dennis Barnett aged 33 born Gravesend, Kent - Fish porter

Wife:

Mary Ann Barnett aged 32 born Bethnal Green

Children:

Dennis aged 9 born Bethnal Green

John aged 6 born Bermondsey

Aunt:

Mrs Hayes aged 75 born Ireland.

The identity of this Mrs Hayes is a mystery. She is presumably the sister of either Catherine or John Barnett, but which is not known. The mysteriously disappearing Catherine Barnett would have been somewhere about 60 in 1881, so it not likely to be her having assumed another identity for unknown reasons.

The second son, Daniel, in 1881 had also moved to Bermondsey and had moved into lodgings:

9 Aldred Street, Bermondsey
Lodger:
Daniel Barnett aged 29 born Middlesex - Fish porter
The head of the household is listed as James Murphy, aged 51, a cab driver.

Joseph himself was also living in lodgings in Horatio Street in Bethnal Green just to the south of Haggerston Park. By chance his younger brother John was visiting him at the time of the census, which aids greatly in verifying that we have the right individual.

1 Horatio Street, London
Head:
George Bailey aged 28 born City of London - General dealer
Wife:
Mary A Bailey aged 26 born St Luke's
Children:
James aged 5 born St Luke's
Lizzie aged 3 born Shoreditch
Alfred aged 1 born Shoreditch
Lodger:
Joseph Barnett aged 22 (Unmarried) born Whitechapel - General labourer
Visitor:
John Barnett aged 20 born Whitechapel - Fish porter

When we come to 1891, we can trace two of the brothers without too much difficulty:

Charles William Mowl Victoria Home No 1, Commercial Street, Whitechapel
Lodger:
Daniel Barnett aged 44 born Whitechapel - Fish porter
and
46 Hanbury Street
Lodger:

John Barnett aged 30 born Whitechapel - General labourer.

However, Joseph himself, like his mother before him, seems to have done a disappearing act! There is no definite sighting of him in the 1891 or 1901 census. I applied a little logic to this situation to see if I could find him. Joseph's birth certificate gives his date of birth as 25th May 1858, so at the time of the 1891 census he would have been 32 years of age, one month away from his 33rd birthday. As always we must be wary of age alone as an identifier as this can be very "fluid" in census records and often varies by a year or two either way. In the census records we have for Joseph, his ages at the times of the censuses are given as follows:

1861 - 3
1871 - 13
1881 - 22

In the 1891 census we would therefore be looking for a Joseph Barnett of 33 or thereabouts. I have searched under variants of the forename (Joseph, Joe, Jos, J. etc) and under the surname (Barnett, Barnet) and possible logical mistranscriptions (Barrett, Bassett, even Parnell). There were a few possible identifications but, without exception, there was one huge stumbling block for all these individuals. All were listed as married, and from the ages of the children listed, it was obvious that the marriage took place well before 1888. The available evidence we have about Barnett offers, as far as I am aware, not the slightest hint that at the time he was living with Kelly that he was married and had fathered children.

All of the above searches were carried out on the premise that Barnett, after the murders, carried on living in London. The next logical step was to extend the same searches as outlined above outside the capital incorporating the added provisos that any individual who seemed a likely identification must be either unmarried or must have married since the time of the murders in late 1888.

All of the above conditions lead to only one individual. This person's surname in the 1891 census (both the index and original enumerator's sheet) was listed as Barnet but this same man's name was listed in 1901 as Barnett. To reiterate I was looking for someone with the following characteristics:

1) His name would be Joseph Barnett or some feasible variant thereof

2) His age would in 1891 be 33 or close thereto

3) If he were married indications are that this would have occurred after November 1888

4) His trade would probably be that of a labourer or of similar status.

5) His place of birth would have been listed as in or near Whitechapel

The only person fulfilling all these criteria was married and was in fact living in Kent. He had one daughter but she was only 11 months old at the time of the marriage (i.e. born May 1890 and conception some time about August 1889) which means that the marriage could well have taken place in 1889. The Kent connection brings us back to the fact that Dennis Barnett, is listed in two census entries as born in Gravesend, Kent. There had apparently been a Kent connection at some stage with the family, but currently that is all we can say on that subject.

The listing in 1891 for this Joseph is as follows:

3 True Briton Alley, Minster in Sheppey, Kent

Head:

Joseph Barnet (sic) aged 33 born Spitalfields - Labourer

Wife:

Catherine Barnet aged 37 born Bridge, Kent

Daughter:

Florence Teresa Barnet aged 11 months born Sheerness, Kent

The 1901 information for this family is as follows:

Yielstead, Stockbury, Kent

Head:

Joseph Barnett aged 44(?) born Spitalfields - Agricultural labourer

Wife:

Catherine Barnett aged 48 born Bridge, Kent

Daughter:

Florence Barnett aged 10 born Sheerness

Did Joseph Barnett marry shortly after the Kelly murder and leave London for Kent? I cannot say that for certain. All I can say is that this

Joseph Barnett living in Kent is the most likely option I have found to date. Bruce Paley's Barnett disappears from the record from the time of the Kelly murder until 1906 when he reappears in Shadwell and resumes his profession of fish porter. Whether this Kent Barnett fills in the missing years I cannot firmly say - but he is the nearest possibility I have yet uncovered.

This all leads us to the inexorable question - why has Barnett proved so popular as a comparatively recent suspect? It must be pointed out that even those who support Barnett's candidacy are divided on just what he stands accused of. Some would give him the mantle for all five murders, but many suggest that he was the killer of Kelly alone.

Before looking at the alleged case against Barnett, we should examine the alibi that Barnett himself gave for the night of the murder. He had been with Kelly earlier in the evening of Thursday, 8th November and left her room in Miller's Court somewhere about 7.45 or 8.00 that evening. When asked about his whereabouts on the night of the murder, the Daily Telegraph of 10th November reported as follows:

"Barnett is a porter at the market close by, and he was able to answer the police that on Thursday night he was at a lodging-house in New-street, Bishopsgate-street, and was playing whist there until half-past twelve, when he went to bed."

The Irish Times of 10 November states:

"Last night he visited her between half-past 7 and 8,and told her he was sorry he had no money to give her. He saw nothing more of her. He was indoors this morning when he heard that a woman had been murdered in Dorset street, but he did not know at first who the victim was. He voluntarily went to the police, who, after questioning him, satisfied themselves that his statements were correct, and therefore released him."

The implication of these two alleged timings is that Barnett was in the lodging house from well before 12.30 a.m. when he retired until after 10.45 as he was "indoors" when he heard of the murder which, even spreading rapidly from mouth to mouth, would have taken quite a while to spread from Dorset Street to Bishopsgate. What is not known and not made explicit from the sources is at what time Barnett actually arose on the morning of the 9th and whether he left the lodging house between waking and hearing about the murder.

Various points are raised in the case against Barnett and we will now look at these in turn:
1) Barnett is described as 5ft 7in in height, aged 30, medium build, fair complexion and moustache. This allegedly matches well various witness descriptions of men who could be the killer. From the available descriptions there are only two, in my opinion, that can be said to match Barnett's physical appearance closely. Joseph Lawende saw a man in the company of a woman he identified from her clothing as Catherine Eddowes shortly before the murder in Mitre Square. This man was described as aged about 30, 5ft 7in to 5ft 8in in height, fair complexion and moustache. Israel Schwartz saw a man assault a woman in Berner Street shortly before the murder of Elizabeth Stride. This man is described as about 30, broad shouldered, 5ft 5in in height, brown hair, fair complexion and small brown moustache. Three men were allegedly seen near Miller's Court in the hours leading up to Kelly's murder, two of them in her company. Neither the blotchy faced man with the carroty moustache seen by Mary Cox, nor the well dressed man seen by George Hutchinson match the description of Barnett. And the man seen by Sarah Lewis outside the lodging house opposite Miller's Court is so vaguely described that no meaningful comparison is possible. Other witness accounts which describe the man seen as Jewish or foreign in appearance have no point of similarity with Barnett. Caroline Maxwell's sighting of Kelly talking to a man outside the Britannia public house varied from the police statement (where he was described as dressed as a market porter) to her inquest testimony (in which he had on dark clothes and a plaid coat.) Maxwell added in her police statement "I was some distance away and am doubtful whether I could identify him." In her inquest testimony this had become the more positive "I could not describe the man." The fact that the man was dressed as a market porter calls to mind that Barnett had worked as both a fish and fruit porter, but whether he would still have been wearing the clothing of that trade some time after he had ceased working in that capacity is questionable.

Also, Maxwell said in her testimony specifically that she knew Barnett. Either the man she saw was not Barnett or she did not wish to identify him. We must not forget that Barnett had also testified, so he would have been sitting there in court as Maxwell testified.

2) Barnett's relationship with Kelly could have explained why the killings ceased with her death. This is based on the supposed motive for Barnett being the Ripper. This runs as follows: Barnett's loss of employment in June or July 1888 meant he was no longer able to support the couple financially, and Kelly had once more resorted to prostitution, of which Barnett strongly disapproved. This line of reasoning argues that the earlier murders were scare tactics to keep Kelly off the streets, and when this failed and the couple split up on the 30th October he finally murdered Kelly in a fit of spurned love. There are certainly indications in Barnett's testimony that he knew Kelly was again working on the streets and that he strongly disapproved. In his police statement he says:

"in consequence of not earning sufficient money and her resorting to prostitution, I resolved on leaving her."

This is modified in his inquest testimony when he says:

"I separated from her on the 30th of October. I left her because she had a person who was a prostitute whom she took in and I objected to her doing so - that was the only reason, not because I was out of work."

He also adds this item of information:

"She had on several occasions asked me to read about the murders - she seemed afraid of some one, she did not express fear of any particular individual, except when she rowed with me but we always came to terms quickly."

The fact that Kelly was curious about the murders is not in itself remarkable as it would have been by this stage in the series still a major topic of conversation and speculation. The ambiguous statement is that she expressed fear of some one, and the only individual to whom this applied was Barnett himself. This part of the evidence, in the more fully reported exchange in the Daily Telegraph, runs as follows:

[Coroner] Have you heard her speak of being afraid of any one ? - Yes; several times. I bought newspapers, and I read to her everything about the murders, which she asked me about.

[Coroner] Did she express fear of any particular individual ? - No, sir. Our own quarrels were very soon over. This shows that the summary of evidence in the inquest papers had conflated two items of testimony into one sentence with an almost certainly unintended double meaning. The inquest papers could be read almost to imply that Kelly feared Barnett on occasion, and the fact this follows immediately upon the question of reading reports about the murders could imply she feared he was the killer. The fuller version as reported in the Telegraph makes it clear that this meaning was neither intended nor could it reasonably be read into what he had actually said.

There is certainly evidence that Kelly and Barnett had argued on occasion of which the broken window was a legacy. Barnett himself admitted that they argued but said any such rows were soon over. There is also contained in the witness statements indications that Kelly was not the easiest woman in the world to live with. Although Barnett himself said "she was as long as she was with me of sober habits," the evidence of other witnesses certainly casts doubt upon this assertion. John McCarthy, their landlord, stated: "I very often saw deceased worse for drink - she was a very quiet woman when sober but noisy when in drink." Mary Ann Cox said that when she saw Kelly at midnight she was "very much intoxicated" and ended her statement with the words "I very often saw deceased drunk". Caroline Maxwell's alleged first sighting of Kelly on the Friday morning describes her in the throes of a bad hangover. Julia Venturney asserted: "She lived with Joe Barnett - she frequently got drunk."

We must also remember the number of witnesses who specifically said they knew Joseph Barnett as well as Kelly. McCarthy and Bowyer, his factotum, would have known the couple comparatively well. Caroline Maxwell, Julia Venturney and Maria Harvey specifically said in their testimonies that they knew Barnett. If Joseph Barnett had been hanging about Miller's Court later than he claimed to have been there, there was a very high chance that he would have been recognised if seen.

The one point at which Barnett changed his story between the statement he made on the day of the murder and the hearing of the inquest, was with regard to his motive for finally separating from Kelly on the 30th October. In his police statement he attributed this to his "not earning sufficient money to give her" and her "resorting to prostitution." At the inquest, three days later, he stated that he left her "because she had a person who was a prostitute whom she took in and I objected to her doing so - that was the only reason, not because I was out of work." I believe this change in his evidence was motivated by trying to save face, both for himself and his dead lover. The fact that he could no longer support Kelly financially must have troubled him in two ways:

1) In that more chauvinistic age he would almost certainly have seen himself as the breadwinner and provider of the household. Of course, in the east End many women worked from financial necessity, but in late Victorian times the man of the household was still definitely seen as the provider and head of the family.

2) More troubling to him, almost certainly, was the fact that financial hardship would force Kelly back into the only profession she knew. How and when Kelly first became involved in prostitution is not known. Barnett blamed it on her cousin in Cardiff when she went to stay there, but this is unprovable. There is certainly ample evidence from the witness statements that Kelly had been working as a prostitute and that Barnett strongly disapproved of her doing so, not unreasonably.

There is also the minor possibility that had Barnett admitted that he had not been working and had in effect been living off the proceeds of Kelly's prostitution, he would have laid himself open to a charge of living off immoral earnings.

To summarise, I cannot see any indication in the available testimony that Barnett would have reacted to Kelly's conduct by resorting to hideous and disfiguring murder. All we can know at this remove in time seems to indicate that he cared deeply about Kelly and tried to do his best for a woman who had a troubled and unsettled past and must have proved difficult and perhaps even violent to live with.

3) The ginger beer bottles found in Miller's Court are linked with the

mention of a ginger beer bottle in the "Dear Boss" letter which was the first to use the nickname "Jack the Ripper." This is a nonsense point on two counts:

1) Ginger beer bottles were a very common container in late Victorian London and would have been reused in a variety of ways. The fact that some were found in Kelly's room is in itself meaningless, as the same would have been true of many abodes in the East End.

2) The "Dear Boss" letter, in my opinion - as well as that of many researchers - has nothing to do with the Whitechapel murderer and was not a product of his hand. Who did write it - whether a journalist or some other unnamed individual - is a lengthy and much debated question, and that debate does not belong here. But even if Barnett were the killer, that would not relate him to this dubious document in any way.

4) The "mystery" of the locked door is also cited as showing that Barnett may well have still been in possession of the key and his use of it to let himself out after having murdered Kelly would explain why the door was locked when the police arrived. In the fuller version of the inquest testimony, Inspector Abberline testified: "An impression has gone abroad that the murderer took away the key of the room. Barnett informs me that it has been missing some time, and since it has been lost they have put their hand through the broken window, and moved back the catch. It is quite easy." There was at least one witness in court who would have known the truth of this statement. Maria Harvey testified that she had stayed with Kelly in her room overnight on the Monday and Tuesday and had spent all Thursday afternoon with her. She must have been aware of the unusual arrangement for gaining access in the absence of a key. It is frustrating that she was not questioned on this matter as she was the one person present who could have verified what Barnett had said. However, as the fact that the door could not be opened became such an issue on the day of the murder, and held the police up until 1.30, a point extensively mentioned at the inquest, it seems odd that Harvey would not have mentioned the presence of a key if it had been available in the days before the murder. I can see no valid reason from the evidence we have for doubting that Barnett's story was the simple truth. He was interviewed for four hours on the day of the

murder and Abberline made a point at the inquest of refuting the idea that there was any mystery attached to the whereabouts of the key.

The final point raised in the allegation that Barnett has a case to answer is his alleged similarity to the F.B.I. profile of the killer. Apart from the many questions raised about the accuracy of such profiling, the portrait produced is, in my opinion, so vague as to apply to many hundreds, if not thousands, of men living in the East End at the time. Also two points raised for consideration are, in my opinion, flawed. The profile says the killer would probably be a white male, 28 to 36 years of age living or working in Whitechapel. This fits Barnett and countless other men living in the area in 1888. The profile asserts the killer would have had an absent or passive father figure - Barnett's father died when he was young, 6 years of age, and his mother mysteriously disappeared from the household. The next point, that "the killer probably had a profession in which he could legally experience his destructive tendencies" is, in my opinion, flawed when applied to Barnett. This idea that filleting dead fish would either have satisfied the dark urges of a homicidal maniac or have prepared him with enough anatomical knowledge to dissect a human corpse is absurd. Apart from that, we must remember that Joseph Barnett was a fish porter, hence his main duty would have been carrying the fish in circular baskets. A distinctive reinforced hat was worn for this duty as these baskets were carried piled on the head. Many of the fish sold at Billingsgate would have been gutted and filleted on the quayside where they were caught before being sent off to market. The next item in the profile claims "the Ripper probably ceased his killing because he was either arrested for some other crime, or felt himself close to being discovered as the killer." Barnett, as stated above, was interviewed for four hours on the day of the murder, at least part of the time, evidently, by Abberline himself. Barnett must have been aware that in the early hours of the investigation he would have been a strong prima facie suspect. He asserted that as soon as he heard in the lodging house where he was staying about the murder he voluntarily went to the police. Abberline raised no doubts about Barnett's testimony, and the Coroner at the inquest made a point of saying to Barnett that he had given his evidence "very well indeed." Hardly the circumstances in which a man would feel himself to be "close to being discovered." The last point of comparison is the other one which I feel is flawed. The profile says the killer is likely to have "some sort of physical defect which was the source of a great deal of frustration or anger." This has given rise to the recent assertion, on the basis of one press report, that Barnett suffered from a condition called echolalia. Echolalia has been depicted as a speech impediment in which the last words of the interlocutor are repeated for no apparent reason.

The condition of echolalia is actually much more complex than this. There are actually two types of the condition - immediate and delayed. The latter type would not apply to the assertion made about Barnett. Delayed echolalia occurs when a phrase is repeated long after exposure to it and usually completely out of context. An example of this is the repetition of the phrase "Who's on first?" by Dustin Hoffman's character in the film "Rain Man." Immediate echolalia itself is subdivided into two categories - interactive and non-interactive. The categories of each type have seen summarised as follows:

Functional categories of immediate echolalia (Prizant & Duchan, 1981).

Category	Description
A. Interactive	
1. Turn taking	1.Utterances used as turn fillers in an alternating verbal exchange.
2. Declarative	2.Utterances labelling objects, actions, or location (accompanied by demonstrative gestures).
3. Yes answer	3.Utterances used to indicate affirmation of a prior utterance.
4. Request	4.Utterances used to request objects or others' actions. Usually involves mitigated echolalia.
B. Noninteractive	
1. Nonfocused	1.Utterances produced with no apparent intent and often in states of high arousal (e.g., fear, pain).
2. Rehearsal	2.Utterances used as a processing aid, followed

by utterance or action indicating comprehension of echoed utterance.

3. Self-regulatory   3.Utterances which serve to regulate one's own actions. Produced in synchrony with motor activity.

Echolalia is commonly associated with autism, it being calculated that up to 75% of persons with autism exhibit echolalia. The condition can also be associated with Tourette's Syndrome and some types of schizophrenia.

However, all this is academic unless we address the central issue of did Joseph Barnett suffer from echolalia? The links in the chain of evidence are, in my opinion, very weak.

1) On the basis of one press report we are told that Barnett repeated words.

2) We assume that this repetition was of the severity and nature to constitute a recognised condition

3) That condition was echolalia.

The fullest account we have of Barnett's actual words is the inquest report from the Daily Telegraph. This is important in that it actually gives the wording of the Coroner's questions as well as Barnett's answers. Having gone through Barnett's testimony in detail, the following is a list of instances when he uses words which occurred in the preceding question:

1) [Coroner] Were you on good terms ? - Yes, on friendly terms

2) [Coroner] Was she, generally speaking, of sober habits ? - When she was with me I found her of sober habits

And that is it! The only examples I can find where Barnett actually echoed a word or words used by the questioner. I hardly think this constitutes a psychological condition or a speech impediment.

To be fair to Barnett, if he were not the killer, we must for a moment ponder the psychological condition in which he would have been at the inquest. He was the focus of press attention in the most notorious case of the day, in the formal, imposing setting of an inquest court, giving intimate and unflattering details about the woman with whom he had lived for a year and half and who only a few days before had been murdered in an appalling and degrading manner. I think a little hesitancy or verbal stumbling on Barnett's part could be forgiven, and, in my opinion, that is why the Coroner commented on the manner in which he had given his evidence, for getting through a harrowing and traumatic experience with a modicum of dignity and lucidity. We may give the Ripper many names - and, indeed, many such have been put forward - but it is my opinion that Joseph Barnett is not one of those names.

Chapter 9

Other Accounts

This chapter will examine some of the oddities which occur in the various reports of the murder of Mary Jane Kelly. There are various strange outcroppings in the story as related in press accounts. Some are clearly in error, others are intriguing but currently not provable. What is amazing is how quickly some of these accounts arose and how detailed and plausible some of the stories are. Some of them gained wide currency but to understand this we must remember that many stories would have been syndicated i.e. an account written by a correspondent in London would have been wired by telegraph countrywide or even worldwide, and any errors or inventions in that account would thereby have been propagated. So, we shall be looking at a variety of accounts that grew from the Kelly case - some plausible, some less so - which appear to have been in error.

1) The location of Kelly's room.

The early reports which described the scene of the murder included certain errors that appeared in a good number of press reports both in the United Kingdom and abroad. The amazing speed with which reports could be forwarded from London is evidenced by the fact that on the 9th of November, the actual day of the murder, reports of the events were published in the Boston Daily Globe, The Washington Evening Star and the Ottawa Free Press. The three most persistent errors appear to be:

1) That Kelly lived on the second floor
2) That Kelly's room faced onto Dorset Street
3) That the name of the court where she lived was Cartin's Court. One report in The Star even refers to the location of her room as McCarthy's Court.

An example of this misinformation can be found in the Boston Daily Globe for the 10th of November:

"A woman, 26 years old, by name Mary Jane Kelly, has lived for four months in the front room on the second floor of a house, up an alley known as Cartin's court. This poor woman was in service a short time ago, but since she came to reside in the court she had been recognized by neighbors as a person who like so many unfortunate members of her sex in the eastern end of the town, has managed to pass a wretched existence by the practice of immorality under the most degrading conditions. Cartin's court faces a small square with a narrow entrance, and is surrounded by squalid lodging-houses with rooms to let to women of this unfortunate class."

An even more bizarre report from the East and West Ham Gazette of the 10th of November claims that Kelly's body was found in a shed. They named the alleyway as Dorset Court:

" At half-past 10 yesterday morning the dead body of a woman, with her head almost severed from her body, was found in an untenanted outhouse or shed in Dorset-court, Dorset-street, Commercial-street, Spitalfields. It had evidently been there for some hours, but several scavengers who were in the court at nine o'clock declare that the body was not there then."

The idea that Kelly's body was found on an upper floor facing the street is actually compounded with a strange story that she did not live in the building but came there with a man who rented a room. This is recounted in the East London Observer of 19th November:

"According to all accounts, the woman who was murdered was not a regular habitué of the place; on the contrary, she was rather well dressed, apparently about twenty-five years of age, and even good looking. As to what time she came to the house on Friday morning, and as to the description of the man who accompanied her, no definite information has been received at the time of writing, thanks to the extreme reticence of the police. This much, however, has been found, that some payment was made by the man for the use of the room; that that payment was received by someone residing in the house; and that the murderer and his victim entered the place in the small hours of Friday morning - between one and two o'clock as near as can be gathered. The couple proceeded to a front room of the upper floor of the house, and it was on a wretched looking piece of furniture that the murder was committed. The inhabitants of the house are not early risers, and it was not till ten o'clock on Friday morning that they even thought to ascertain the reason why the door of that front room was locked."

The account of the same day from the Ottawa Citizen is one which mentions the actual floor on which Kelly's room was allegedly located:
"It has been learned that a man respectfully dressed accosted the victim and offered her money. They went to her lodgings on the second floor of the Dorset street house."

The source of these errors would appear to have been an original account drafted by a reporter who visited the scene and interviewed locals. This, or a similar report also of a very early date, would seem to be the origin of the allegation that Kelly was married to a man named Lawrence. The most specific item which is in error is that the name of the court was Cartin's Court. There does not appear to have been a real court in London at this time of that name - or at any other time, come to that. There is no such road in the 1891 or 1901 census, nor does the Ordnance Survey map for this area of 1894 show any such name. My guess would be that this was a local nickname for Miller's Court. The court was obviously too narrow to park carts and barrows in - as was done in Castle Alley, scene of a later murder attributed by some to the Ripper - but there may in the past have been some connection to carters or carting. There is another possibility. The houses in Miller's Court were known colloquially as "McCarthy's Rents." It is possible that a previous owner and landlord may have been named Cartin. As an indicator, there were 30 individuals in the 1881 census of the surname Cartin, the majority of whom were of Irish origin.

2) Mary Jane Kelly had a son.
The story that Kelly had a young son living with her is both very early in origin and also becomes incredibly detailed very quickly. The outline of the story is that Kelly had a young son, whose age seems to vary from seven to eleven years old, living with her. On the night of the murder a man came to her room and she sent the child to stay with a neighbour. For once we have a quoted source for the earliest occurrence of this story. On the 9th of November, the day of the murder, an account

appeared in The Star which specifically says that the details were told to the Star reporter by the inhabitants of the lodging houses in Dorset Street. This includes the first mention of Kelly's child:

"But from the startled inhabitants of the lodging-houses in Dorset-street a Star man got a few details. The victim is a woman who went by the name of Mary Jane and she lived in the room in which she has been murdered, with a man and her little son - about 10 or 11 years old."

The fuller version of the story of the boy appeared in the Times of the following day, 10th November:

"Another account gives the following details: Kelly had a little boy, aged about 6 or 7 years living with her, and latterly she had been in narrow straits, so much so that she is reported to have stated to a companion that she would make away with herself, as she could not bear to see her boy starving. There are conflicting statements as to when the woman was last seen alive, but that upon which most reliance appears to be placed is that of a young woman, an associate of the deceased, who states that at about half-past 10 o'clock on Thursday night she met the murdered woman at the corner of Dorset-street, who said to her that she had no money and, if she could not get any, would never go out any more but would do away with herself. Soon afterwards they parted, and a man, who is described as respectably dressed, came up, and spoke to the murdered woman Kelly and offered her some money. The man then accompanied the woman to her lodgings, which are on the second floor, and the little boy was removed from the room and taken to a neighbour's house. Nothing more was seen of the woman until yesterday morning, when it is stated that the little boy was sent back into the house, and the report goes, he was sent out subsequently on an errand by the man who was in the house with his mother. There is no direct confirmation of this statement."

The oddest mention of Kelly having a child comes from the Star of the 10th of November. After leaving Kelly, Barnett went to live at Buller's Lodging House, 25 New Street. The Star reporter tracked Barnett down to a public house near his lodgings and interviewed him. This interview appears to quote Barnett as confirming that Kelly had a child:

"JOE BARNETT'S STATEMENT.

In a public-house close by Buller's the reporter succeeded later on in finding Barnett, who is an Irishman by parentage and a Londoner by birth. He had lived with her for a year and a half, he said, and should not have left her except for her violent habits. She was a Limerick woman by birth, he says, but had lived in Dublin for some time. She went by the name of Mary Jane, but her real name was Marie Jeanette. He knew nothing about her proceedings since he left her, except that his brother met her on the Thursday evening and spoke to her. He himself had been taken by the police down to Dorset-street, and had been kept there for two hours and a half. He saw the body by peeping through the window.

To our reporter Barnett said he and the deceased were very happy and comfortable together until another woman came to sleep in their room, to which he strongly objected. Finally, after the woman had been there two or three nights he quarrelled with the woman whom he called his wife and left her. The next day, however, he returned and gave Kelly money. He called several other days and gave her money when he had it. On Thursday night he visited her between half-past seven and eight, and told her he was sorry he had no money to give her. He saw nothing more of her. She used occasionally to go to the Elephant and Castle district to visit a friend who was in the same position of life as herself. Kelly had a little boy, aged about six or seven years, living with her."

Apart from the question of Kelly's child, this statements contains other matters of interest:

Barnett's assertion that Kelly had lived in Dublin fits with the area of Ireland from which the family of Mary Ann Kelly, of Flint, was listed as originating.

In this account there is yet another motive quoted by Barnett for leaving Kelly, namely her violent habits.

He specifically says that his brother had met and spoken with Kelly on Thursday evening, the 8th. This fits the assertion of Maurice Lewis that he saw Kelly with "Danny," presumably Daniel Barnett.

We do not have a definite time for Barnett going to the police from the lodging house in which he was staying. However, his assertion that he saw the body by peeping through the window suggests this may have been before the door was forced at 1.30 p.m.

What are we to make of this? There is no definite record of Kelly having a child. But, there again, as we have seen, there is no definite record of Kelly doing anything! In the light of Kelly's colourful past and her time spent on the streets it is no means beyond the bounds of possibility that at some stage she had fallen pregnant or had even given birth to a child. However, there is not one shred of evidence from the inquest or any statement by a witness that Kelly had a child living with her at the time of her death or shortly before. The attribution of the statement to Barnett that this had been the case could be the result of some creative journalism, appending a supposed item of information which had appeared in the press to Barnett's words to give them a spurious legitimacy.

3) Kelly was pregnant at the time of her death.

This allegation is an object lesson in how supposed facts can become embedded in the fabric of Ripper studies and passed from hand to hand - or from pen to pen - until they become canonised and accepted as established fact. A number of major books prior to the 1980s stated that Mary Kelly was pregnant at the time she was murdered. Tom Cullen even put a time on this, saying that she was three months pregnant.

The mystery with this story is how and when it arose. There is absolutely nothing in the contemporary evidence or press reports to suggest that Kelly was carrying a child. I have been unable to trace when this supposed fact was first mentioned, but it must have been some not inconsiderable time after the murder. The authoritative document to resolve this matter is the post mortem report by Dr. Thomas Bond, which was not available for study until 1987, when it, along with other important material relating to the Whitechapel murders was returned anonymously to the police authorities. Dr. Bond did not, as has been implied in some sources, specifically say that Kelly was not pregnant. His only mention of the uterus was to say that it had been found lodged under the victim's head, along with other organs. The logic in the case for dismissing Kelly's pregnancy is that if Kelly had been pregnant, Bond would surely have mentioned it. But how confidently can we put words into the mouth of a doctor at this remove in time? It would seem to be a very important point but we cannot be utterly certain that Bond would have mentioned the fact. In my opinion, the balance of probability is that he would have drawn attention to the fact, and Kelly was probably not carrying a child at the time of her death.

4) Members of Kelly's family.

The only information we have about Kelly's family background is that which was supplied by Joseph Barnett. One question that has been posed by some researchers is why members of Kelly's family did not come forward either to identify the body or at least to attend the funeral? Certainly in the cases of some of the former victims, family members came forward or were traced by the police and gave inquest evidence. If the outline details of Kelly's life, and the name that she used, were true, her family would have had difficulty in avoiding exposure to the details in the press.

There are some press reports that her family had been contacted and were on their way to London for the funeral, but in the event no family members attended her interment. But there is one more detailed and intriguing report which appeared in The Star of the 12th of November. This is in the context of another alleged interview with Joseph Barnett:

"Some further details as to the woman's antecedents are coming out. Joseph Barnett, the man she lived with in the room in which she was murdered said: - "When she was but little over 16 years of age she married a collier, but I do not remember his name. He was killed in an explosion in the mine, and then Marie went to Cardiff with her cousin. Thence she went to France, but remained only a short time. Afterwards she lived in a fashionable house in the West-end of London; but drifted from the West-end to the East-end, where she took lodgings in Pennington-street. Her father came from Wales, and tried to find her there; but, hearing from her companions that he was looking for her, Marie kept out of the way. A brother in the Second Battalion Scots Guards came to see her once, but beyond that she saw none of her relations, nor did she correspond with them. When she was in Pennington-street a man named Morganstone lived with her, and subsequently a man named

Joseph Fleming passed as her husband."

These allegations that her father came seeking her in Pennington Street and her brother visited her once, I have not seen elsewhere and cannot make any judgement about their reliability. It may be significant that the only relation who allegedly visited is the only one of her siblings mentioned by Barnett by name. This brother in the Scots Guards was named by Barnett in his inquest testimony as Henry, also known as Johnto. The episode of her father seeking her and her keeping out of his way does have the possible ring of truth of either her shame in what she had become or of a family rift which drove her away. But this does not constitute proof and this story attributed to Barnett remains just another unproven tale.

5) The "other man".

There is a report which I have so far found in only one source which alleges that Kelly was seen with an unknown man away from Miller's Court shortly before the murder. The source of this story was Mrs. Carthy, Kelly's former landlady in Breezer's Hill, off the Ratcliff Highway. After the murder on the 9th of November, Mrs. Carthy was traced and interviewed regarding what she knew about Kelly. One section of this article is tantalisingly interesting:

"The unfortunate victim is described as being a woman about 25 years of age, 5ft 7in in height, rather stout, with blue eyes, fair complexion, and a very good head of hair. She had two false teeth in her upper jaw. She was known to be leading a gay life in the neighbourhood of Aldgate. Mrs. Carthy states that the deceased when she left her place went to live with a man in the building trade, and who she (Mrs. Carthy) believed would have married her. She, however, was awakened by Kelly some short time ago at two o'clock in the morning, when she was with a strange man, and asked for a bed for the night. On that occasion Mrs. Carthy asked the deceased if she was not living with the man who took her from the neighbourhood. She replied in the negative, and explained her position. From this time she was never seen in the neighbourhood."

Now, it all depends on what Mrs. Carthy meant by the phrase "a short time ago." Does this mean days, weeks or months? This interview was published on the 17th November, 1888, in a provincial UK paper from east Kent entitled the Thanet Advertiser. So, shortly before that time, Kelly turned up at her old haunt in Breezer's Hill with an unknown man asking for a bed. There can be no question of misidentification of Kelly, as Mrs. Carthy had been her landlady and knew her well. The man could not have been Joseph Fleming as it seems apparent that Mrs. Carthy knew him as well. The unknown factor is whether the ex landlady knew Joseph Barnett, with whom Kelly was by that time certainly living. But to theorise that the unknown man was Barnett is nonsensical. The couple by this time had been living for almost a year and a half at Miller's Court. Why would they walk all the way to Breezer's Hill (a not inconsiderable distance) to get a bed for the night? It makes no sense. The other thing which Mrs. Carthy does not reveal is whether or not she allowed Kelly and the unknown man to stay the night. Who he was and when this happened are yet two more unknowns in the Kelly story.

6) Visits from a past lover?

It seems that Kelly's relationship with Joseph Fleming, the plasterer, was particularly close. Mrs. Carthy, in the article quoted above, said that she thought that Fleming would have married Kelly. Although Carthy does not refer to him by name, her statements that Kelly went to live with him from Breezer's Hill and also that he was in the building trade, makes this identification pretty certain. There are also fragmentary hints that Fleming carried on visiting Kelly even after she was living with Barnett, who observed that she was "very fond of him."

Unfortunately, the section of Barnett's testimony dealing with her relationships with Morganstone and Fleming is extremely muddled. This can be explained by the fact which Barnett himself stated that he did not know the order in which these relationships occurred. The section in question, which describes Kelly's movements after she returned from France, reads:

"She came back and lived in Ratcliffe Highway for some time, she did not tell me how long. Then she was living near Stepney Gas Works. Morganstone was the man she lived with there. She did not tell me how long she lived there. She told me that in Pennington Street she lived with a Morganstone, and with Joseph Flemming, she was very fond of him. He was a mason's plasterer. He lived in Bethnal Green Road. She told me all this, but I do not know which she lived with last. Flemming used to visit her."

The fuller version as printed in the Daily Telegraph throws a little more light on this period in Kelly's life:

"She returned to England, and went to Ratcliffe-highway. She must have lived there for some time. Afterwards she lived with a man opposite the Commercial Gas Works, Stepney. The man's name was Morganstone.

[Coroner] Have you seen that man ? - Never. I don't know how long she lived with him.

[Coroner] Was Morganstone the last man she lived with ? - I cannot answer that question, but she described a man named Joseph Fleming, who came to Pennington-street, a bad house, where she stayed. I don't know when this was. She was very fond of him. He was a mason's plasterer, and lodged in the Bethnal-green-road.

[Coroner] Was that all you knew of her history when you lived with her? - Yes. After she lived with Morganstone or Fleming - I don't know which one was the last - she lived with me."

This seems to make it clear that she never actually lived with Fleming but he used to come and visit her when she was living at Pennington Street. Breezer's Hill, where Kelly lodged with Mrs Carthy, was a short thoroughfare that connected George Street, the western end of the former Ratcliff Highway, and Pennington Street. As Mrs Carthy seemed to know a substantial amount about Fleming and his relationship with Kelly, I would guess that this Pennington Street address where he visited Kelly was actually the Carthy house in Breezer's Hill. In the abridged form of Barnett's testimony as contained in the inquest papers, his simple statement "Flemming used to visit her", which could have indicated that he came visiting to Miller's Court after she was living with Barnett, now seems more likely to refer to the time when she was living at Breezer's Hill.

The other source for information about Kelly's relationship with Fleming is Julia Venturney. In her police statement she stated:

"She (Kelly) told me she was very fond of another man named Joe, and he had often ill-used her because she cohabited with Joe (Barnett)."

In the deposition from the inquest papers, this becomes:

"Deceased told me she was fond of another man named Joe who used to come and see her and give her money. I think he was a costermonger - she said she was very fond of him."

Again, this is infuriatingly ambiguous. Does the phrase that this man "used to come and see her and give her money" refer back to the time before Kelly lived with Barnett, or was Venturney saying that Fleming (to whom this other "Joe" must surely refer) still visited Kelly after she moved into Miller's Court? And did he give her money because he was very fond of her, or for some other reason? When we looked at Hutchinson, we saw the possibility that he was a casual client of Kelly's - did the same still apply to Fleming? Barnett specifically says he never met Morganstone - he does not make the same statement about Fleming. So we cannot know if the two ever met. But the statement of Venturney that he (Fleming) ill used Kelly because she was living with Barnett (either at Miller's Court or at one of their earlier lodgings) does confirm that there was continued contact between Kelly and Fleming after she took up with Barnett.

Fleming is an intriguing character in that the various statements about him tell us the following:

1) He wanted to marry Kelly

2) Kelly was "very fond" of him

3) Contact between Kelly and Fleming was maintained at least for a time after she started living with Barnett

4) He "ill used" Kelly because she was living with Barnett - whether this was physical or verbal is not known, but my guess would be the former.

How and why the relationship finally ended between the two is not known, nor is the date when they last met before Kelly's death. Another intriguing aspect is whether or not the police made any efforts - and indeed possibly succeeded - in tracing Fleming and interviewing him. I would have thought that a man who had been very close to the deceased, was jealous of the man she was currently living with and had physically abused her, was someone the police would have been eager to speak with. There is no surviving evidence that the police traced him, or made any effort to do so, but that, of course, does not definitively mean that such a search was not undertaken. Fleming, however, remains a man about whom we would like to know much more.

Chapter 10

Mary Kelly Keeps Busy

Of the five generally accepted victims of the Whitechapel murderer, Mary Kelly has generated more attention and more speculation than any other. This is, in my opinion, for two mains reasons:

1) Researching the lives of the other four "canonical" victims proved comparatively straightforward in that they were unequivocally traceable as individuals in the available documentation. This is not to downplay or underestimate the heroic efforts of those researchers who have revealed so much about these unfortunate women, their backgrounds and their descendants. In this context mention must be made of Neal Stubbings and his series of fascinating publications about the lives and backgrounds of the victims. However, it must also be pointed out that Kelly is not actually unique among the alleged victims in that the background of Alice McKenzie, who was murdered in Castle Alley in July 1889 has proved almost equally impervious.

2) One question that has perennially fascinated researchers and writers is - why did the murders stop? The general observation is that killers of the supposed type of the Whitechapel murderer do not just stop killing - they have, by some means, to be stopped. The usual list of ways in which the killings may have stopped after November 1888 are suicide, the death of the killer by some other means, his incarceration in a prison or asylum for some unrelated offence or his emigration to another country. However, another method of explaining why the killings stopped with Kelly was to adopt the logical position that Kelly was the ultimate target of the killer all along and, thus, with her death his "mission" was complete.

The main pitfall with any theory of this type is that the researcher cannot know the motive of the Whitechapel killer, which must be in any event a huge leap either of faith or of speculation. A lively debate took place at the time of the murders about the killer's motive for perpetrating these ghastly deeds, and that debate is still ongoing and still unresolved. Can the thought processes and the motives of a mind which was evidently, in whatever way, profoundly disturbed be understood in terms of everyday logic?

The necessary outcome of any theory which places Kelly as the ultimate goal of the killer's attentions requires her to have played a special and pivotal role which focussed the murderer's attention upon her. The best known examples of this type of theory are as follows:

1) The Mystery of Jack the Ripper by Leonard Matters (1929)
This book, described as the first full length treatment of the subject in the English language, is allegedly based on the confessions of a Dr. Stanley who died in Buenos Aires. He had earlier in his life been a successful physician in the West End of London, patronised by a wealthy clientele. He had a much loved son, Herbert, in whom he invested much hope and ambition. His son met Mary Kelly on Boat Race night, 1886, and contracted syphilis from her. The dying son told his father of Kelly and, after his beloved boy's death, Dr. Stanley descended upon the East End and sought out Kelly and her associates and killed. He then wandered various parts of the world until he settled in Argentina in 1901, where he finally died in about 1918.

This story has been generally decried by writers and researchers on the subject. It is difficult to give an opinion in that none of Matters' sources are known or can be examined. The alleged newspaper confession on which the book was ultimately based has never been traced and in the absence of any supporting evidence judgement has at the very least to be reserved. Other elements in the story, such as syphilis proving fatal in barely two years, simply do not stand up to scrutiny and cast serious doubts on the whole tale.

2) The Royal Conspiracy theory (1975 and ongoing)
The history of the Royal Conspiracy theory is an astonishing tale in its own right. The name Jack the Ripper has passed into the vernacular and become more a feature of folklore than of historical fact and research. Many people who know the name have only a vague idea of the facts behind the myth. That is not intended as a criticism, for these good folk,

unlike us obsessives who dissect and fuss over the case for any new titbit, probably lead very full and satisfying lives! What is surprising is how quickly and how solidly the Royal Conspiracy has passed into common currency as the accepted solution to the case. Many people to whom I have spoken, usually long suffering friends and family members who are only too aware of my long standing interest in the case, commonly say things such as "Well, what's all the fuss about? I thought they'd solved that years ago?" "It was something to do with the Royal family, wasn't it?" When it is pointed out that the earliest Royal connection of any sort dates back to 1970 and the article published by Thomas Stowell, and the full blown story did not hit the headlines until 1976 with Stephen Knight's book "Jack the Ripper - The Final Solution", I have found this meets with universal surprise. It is assumed that a theory which, for whatever reason, has become so firmly entrenched in the common consciousness must have been around for a very long time.

In some ways the Royal Conspiracy is like the Hydra - if one head is cut off, not only does the beast not die, but two more rear up to take its place! Within the present book I have neither the space (nor, if the truth be told, the inclination) to relate the various incarnations of the Royal Conspiracy theory in great detail, but only in outline to set the alleged role of Mary Kelly in context. In its best known form the theory alleges that Prince Albert Victor, later the Duke of Clarence, under the informal tutelage of Walter Sickert, met and fell in love with a young lady of humble background, Annie Crook. Some form of marriage service was carried out and a daughter, Alice Margaret, was born to the couple in 1886. Mary Kelly acted as nurse to the child. The authorities found about this liaison and child, the result being a raid on Cleveland Street. where Annie Crook had lived and worked, and the Prince and the shop girl were made away with. Kelly and her East End associates, saw an opportunity and began to blackmail the authorities, threatening to reveal what they knew of the scandal. A plot, orchestrated by various high ranking Freemasons, was put in place for a coterie of killers (whose identities change over time depending which form of the theory you read) killed off the women in ritualistic ways, culminating with the death of the mainstay of the blackmail plot, Kelly herself.

Any structure, physical or intellectual, is only as sure as the foundations on which it is built. The two wellsprings from which the Royal Conspiracy theory emerged were:

1) The 1970 article by Thomas Stowell. This was allegedly based on private papers of Sir William Gull, papers which no other researcher has seen, before or since. Stowell identified his suspect only by the letter "S". Not only did he not mention Prince Albert Victor, he positively denied during the press furore that followed his article that the Prince was the suspect he intended to bring to public attention. Stowell himself died very shortly after the publication of his article and all his notes and research material were destroyed by family members. Therefore, we simply cannot judge the strength of Stowell's claims in the light of his own denials of any Royal connection, the non emergence of his source material and the destruction of his own researches. It should be noted that Kelly merited no mention or special note in the outline put forward by Stowell.

2) The first intimation of the more fully developed Royal theory was aired on the television series "Jack the Ripper," shown in 1973. This featured an interview with Joseph Gorman, or, as he styled himself, Joseph Sickert. The fully developed theory, based on the statements of Joseph emerged in the book "Jack the Ripper - The Final Solution." The various allegations and refutations that this book aroused are too lengthy to discuss here and can be more than adequately studied elsewhere. Suffice it so say that the book and its aftermath attracted huge attention and more than a few indications that the research was not as adequately grounded as one would wish to seriously argue such a theory.

Joseph Gorman/Sickert later refuted that part of the book which related to the Whitechapel crimes, but stood by the centrepiece of his account - that he was the son of Alice Margaret Crook and Walter Sickert. However, another book based on Gorman's assertions later emerged in 1991 in the shape of "The Ripper and the Royals" by Melvyn Fairclough. This not only included substantially the same Ripper scenario but introduced certain new elements. The line up of killers had now changed and included Lord Randolph Churchill, it was alleged that Prince Albert Victor had not actually died when supposed (in 1892) but had survived, secreted away. A new piece of alleged evidence was also brought forward in the shape of the supposed diary of Frederick Abberline. Kelly's role in this incarnation was as follows:- it was alleged she was nanny to Annie Crook, worked at Cleveland Street, took the young Alice Crook to the East End and concocted, with the other women, the blackmail plot. This book claims that Kelly told the story of the Prince, his liaison and the child to her cronies and they came up with the idea of blackmail. The demand was originally sent to Walter Sickert but made its way to the hands of the Prime Minister, Lord Salisbury. It was this that set the whole ghastly train of events in motion.

Personally, I find it difficult to make any meaningful comment on the Royal Conspiracy theory in its many forms as it is impossible to form an objective assessment of the reliability of the sources on which the theory is based. The theory is like shifting sand, forever twisting and changing form before your eyes. So I really do not find myself in a position to make any comment on the truthfulness of any of the assertions contained in the theories that have gone under the heading of Royal conspiracy. My instinct, for what it is worth, is that the theory is deeply flawed and in all probability substantially untrue, but lack of any substantiating evidence that can be examined makes this an impossible contention to prove conclusively. Certain aspects, such as the fate of Annie Crook after 1888, can be shown from census data to be almost certainly wrong, and severe doubt has been cast on the provenance of the Abberline diary. But the central story was so much the product of one man's account that it all rests on the reliability of his claims, which now, since the sad death of Joseph Gorman/Sickert recently, cannot be tested or investigated.

My nomination for the most far fetched depiction of Mary Kelly and her role in the story would have to go not to a book, but to the film "From Hell." In this version of the story, Kelly is a feisty, very Celtic denizen of Whitechapel. The full regalia of the Royal conspiracy is present but that is the least of the flights of fancy. Kelly falls in love with Abberline who secretes her away, there is no mention of Joseph Barnett, Kelly not only survives the killing in Miller's Court but ends up in an idyllic cottage by the sea bringing up the young Alice Crook! Mind you, in a film which depicts Frederick Abberline as a widowed, psychic, drug fiend who dies shortly after the murders in the arms of Sergeant Godley can hardly be relied upon for historical reliability. Ironically I did enjoy the film, and some of the set piece reconstructions are very well done. It is a rattling good yarn as long as it is taken on its own terms, that is having no basis whatever in the historical facts of the case.

Chapter 11

Closing Words

What have we learned about Mary Jane Kelly, last generally accepted victim of the Whitechapel murderer? Are we any closer to any definite knowledge about her life or background? Sadly, almost certainly not. Our searches can only lead us to one certain conclusion - that major parts of the account of Kelly's life as related by Joseph Barnett are in error or are deliberate fabrication. If the latter is the case then it is not possible to say whether the invention was on the part of Kelly herself or of Barnett. However, there are details from other witnesses that suggest that at least parts of Barnett's version of Kelly's life were told by Kelly herself.

Mrs. Carthy confirms the relationship between Kelly and Joseph Fleming, as does the testimony of Julia Venturney. There is a press story concerning the mysterious Mrs. Buki with whom Kelly lodged near the Ratcliff Highway prior to becoming a tenant of Mrs. Carthy. Mrs. Buki allegedly went with Kelly to the fancy house in the West End to collect some of her (Kelly's) belongings. The article in the Thanet Advertiser of the 17th of November, 1888, summarises this period of Kelly's life as follows:

" Her experience of the East End appears to have begun with a woman who resided in one of the thoroughfares off Ratcliff Highway, now known as St. George's street. This person appears to have received Kelly direct from her West End home, for she had not been very long with her when, it is stated, both women went to the French "lady's" residence and demanded her box which contained numerous dresses of a costly description. Kelly at last indulged in intoxicants, it is stated, to an extent which made her an unwelcome friend. From St. George's street she went to lodge with Mrs. Carthy at Breezer's Hill, Pennington street."

Presumably, for this information to be forthcoming, the elusive Mrs. Buki, or whatever the correct rendition of her name, must have been traced and interviewed but she, unlike Mrs. Carthy, is not quoted directly. The one press article that names Mrs. Buki, was in The Star of the 12th of November and relates the same incident of collecting the dresses from the house in the West End:

"By some means, however, at present not exactly clear, she suddenly drifted into the East-end. Her first experiences of the East-end appear to have commenced with Mrs. Buki, who resided in one of the thoroughfares off Ratcliff-highway, now known as St. George's-street. Both women went to the French lady's residence, and demanded Kelly's box, which contained numerous costly dresses. From Mrs. Buki's place, Kelly went to lodge with Mrs. Carthy, at Breezer's-hill, Pennington-street."

This same article also contains this item of information:

"It appears from inquiries made at Carmarthen and Swansea, that after leaving the former place for the latter, Kelly, who was then only 17 years of age, entered the service of a Mrs. Rees, who stands committed to the next assizes on a charge of procuring abortion, and who is the daughter of a medical man formerly resident at Carmarthen."

This would indeed be a useful lead to follow, but sadly this rumour was quashed the very same day in a press account in the Cambria Daily Leader, which reads as follows:

"It is stated in the 'Western Mail' that the murdered woman Kelly was at one time a servant with Mrs. Rees (daughter of the late Dr. Hopkins), in Trafalgar Terrace, Swansea. We are asked to say that this is not true."

There are also a number of references to Kelly having a Welsh connection, one unnamed young woman even asserting that she spoke Welsh. One of the most interesting references to Kelly's Welsh background appears in a press article in the Daily News of the 12th of November, 1888. An interview was carried out with an unnamed City missionary, and he had this to say about his acquaintance with Kelly:

"I knew the poor girl who has just been killed, and to look at, at all events, she was one of the smartest, nicest looking women in the neighbourhood. We have had her at some of our meetings, and a companion of hers was one we rescued. I know that she has been in correspondence with her mother. It is not true, as it has been stated, that she is a Welshwoman. She is of Irish parentage, and her mother, I believe, lives in Limerick. I used to hear a good deal about the letters from her mother there. You would not have supposed if you had met her in the street that she belonged to the miserable class she did, as she was always neatly and decently dressed and looked quite nice and respectable." Again, this does not prove a Limerick connection, only that this information came from Kelly and not from Barnett's imagination. It is not clear if the letters from Kelly's mother were shown to the missionary or their contents just described, but it does add some weight to the Irish connection.

We have no certain knowledge of Kelly, only hints and possibilities. Finally, all that can be said is this: if the name of the girl who died in Miller's Court was Mary Kelly, the nearest we have yet found is Mary Ann Kelly, of Irish parentage, of Irish birth herself, whose family had resided briefly in Carnarvon and then moved to Flint. It is not possible to say this is THE Mary Kelly - only that it is the closest match so far found. If, invoking another possibility, one of the things Kelly lied about was her name and it was nothing like Mary Jane Kelly, then the chances of ever finding definite information about her are non existent. Maybe she will remain forever a lady of mystery - who knows? It is the dream of many researchers that one day in the proverbial dusty attic or long forgotten drawer, something will emerge that will cast new light, startling light on this obsessive mystery. But in the light of the Gull papers, the Abberline diary, the Maybrick diary and the Maybrick watch and the heated furore they have engendered, would such an object ever be accepted? In this age of scepticism and entrenched opinion, what would indeed constitute proof?

All we can say is that the woman known as Mary Jane Kelly now sleeps at Leytonstone Cemetery, more thought on in death than she ever was in life. Rest in peace, young lady, whoever you are ...

THE END

Printed in the United Kingdom
by Lightning Source UK Ltd.
121104UK00001B/99